Manage Your Project Portfolio

Increase Your Capacity and Finish More Projects

Manage Your Project Portfolio

Increase Your Capacity and Finish More Projects

Johanna Rothman

The Pragmatic Bookshelf

Raleigh, North Carolina   Dallas, Texas

To anyone who's ever been asked to focus
on more than one project at a time.

And, to Mark, Shaina, and Naomi,
who help me realize what is most important.

Many of the designations used by manufacturers and sellers to distinguish their products are claimed as trademarks. Where those designations appear in this book, and The Pragmatic Programmers, LLC was aware of a trademark claim, the designations have been printed in initial capital letters or in all capitals. The Pragmatic Starter Kit, The Pragmatic Programmer, Pragmatic Programming, Pragmatic Bookshelf and the linking *g* device are trademarks of The Pragmatic Programmers, LLC.

Every precaution was taken in the preparation of this book. However, the publisher assumes no responsibility for errors or omissions, or for damages that may result from the use of information (including program listings) contained herein.

Our Pragmatic courses, workshops, and other products can help you and your team create better software and have more fun. For more information, as well as the latest Pragmatic titles, please visit us at

http://www.pragprog.com

Printed in the United States of America.

ISBN-10: 1-934356-29-8
ISBN-13: 978-1-934356-29-6
Printed on acid-free paper.
P1.0 printing, July 2009
Version: 2009-7-17

While many books focus only on tools and methodologies, Johanna highlights the importance of the critical but often overlooked "soft skills"—trust, influence, negotiation, collaboration—in successful portfolio management. Her approaches are extremely flexible and easily adapted to various life cycles as well as to the culture of your company and team. This book is a must-read for all software development management (and read *Manage It!* first)!

▶ **Ellen R. Salisbury**
   Managing director, Cambridge West Ventures

Juggling competing priorities is what managers are paid to do, but few get the coaching they need to do it well. *Manage Your Project Portfolio* brings expert coaching within reach.

▶ **Dave W. Smith**
   Software development coach

Johanna offers us a down-to-earth pragmatic book on portfolio management. Her conversational style is very engaging. When I picked up the book, I couldn't put it down until I read it cover to cover. She anticipated many of my questions and provides practical answers. This book is filled with solid advice on all aspects of project portfolio management for the individual as well as the enterprise. It belongs on the bookshelf of anyone serious about delivering business value through good portfolio management practices.

▶ **Bob Wysocki**
   President, Enterprise Information Insights

You need to read Johanna Rothman's *Manage Your Project Portfolio*. If you are a confirmed "agileist," you will see how core agile principles have been used to deal with the value an organization expects from its projects. If you are a traditional PMO professional, you will find the insights and points of reference are uncomfortably familiar, because the examples and the outcomes she presents come from her (and our) experiences. Take note of the lessons learned in getting things done, and you should be able to avoid the fate of your colleagues who didn't take the time to read this book.

▶ **Mike Dwyer**
   Principal agile coach, BigVisible Solutions, Inc.

What Readers Are Saying About
Manage Your Project Portfolio

If you leave the office with more projects than you started the day with, this book is for you. This isn't an abstract or theoretical book; Johanna offers practical advice that will help you manage your project portfolio—whether you are a team lead, a middle manager, or a senior executive.

▶ **Esther Derby**
  Author and consultant, Esther Derby Associates, Inc.

At last! Now, we can get serious about extending an agile approach beyond individual projects and begin to extract further value from our agile programs and portfolios. Johanna's book lays out many ways to manage your portfolio—agile or otherwise—and will give you, the manager, the practical tools to apply agile principles beyond the project. Managers in the field will be relieved to be able to get crucial insights from a thought leader in the agile space, and I believe this book will take its place among the best in the field.

▶ **Sanjiv Augustine**
  President, LitheSpeed
  Author, Managing Agile Projects

The hardest thing about managing an agile enterprise is prioritizing across projects. Johanna's book shows how to do this, and it should be on every manager's desk.

▶ **Dan Rawsthorne, PhD**
  Certified Scrum trainer, Danube Technologies

Businesses improve (and profit) by finishing projects, not starting them. In this book Johanna Rothman clearly shows managers how, by making just a few simple changes, they can finish more projects and make considerably more money. This is an important book—a book that should be read by every manager.

▶ **Clarke Ching**
  Theory of constraints consultant, SpiceUpIT.com

Contents

Foreword by Ron Jeffries

Quite often I have the chance to visit a team to help management figure out why they're not making much progress. When I get there, I find a small team working on more projects than they have people. The good news is that now I know what the problem is. The bad news is that I have to explain to management that what they're doing is causing the problem they're complaining about.

Johanna's book is about this issue, including how to identify it and how to resolve it.

I believe that inside every complex solution is a simple solution trying to get out, and I'm very pleased to find that Johanna begins with simple ways to understand our collection of work. Better yet, she returns to those simple approaches again and again. Yes, we have hard decisions and difficult communication with our peers and colleagues ahead of us. To make those communications work, we need to understand the situation and express it clearly. Johanna helps us do that.

No matter where in the organization you find yourself, you'll recognize situations in Johanna's book that are familiar. Then she'll use that familiar context to take you to a new level of understanding of what to do when that sort of thing happens again. There's nothing better than someone who shows she understands your situation and then shows you what you can do to make it better.

Johanna tells us that there are three things to do with each project as we consider our portfolio: we can commit to the project, we can kill it, or we can transform it. Have you seen projects that don't deserve to die but that hang around not coming to life? Maybe they need to be considered at the portfolio level and be transformed. There are definitely some like that in my past! Where was this book when I really needed it?

Then we are shown how to rank the remaining projects, and very eloquently Johanna reminds us of a number of ranking dimensions, including why sometimes those orphan internal projects are among the most important ones to do. She describes several ways to approach ranking. It's likely one of them is right for you, and if not, you can mix and match from the approaches in the book.

Throughout the book, Johanna gives us stories from her own experiences and stories from the experiences of others. She weaves those stories into a consistent, growing understanding that is compelling and easy to understand. Each step along the way, she gives us things to try—things that fit right in with the current chapter's ideas.

The book moves forward steadily, reminding us to collaborate so that the decisions will be better...and better accepted. We learn how and when to iterate and evolve on our portfolio. We learn why and how to stabilize it, what to measure under differing circumstances, and what not to measure as well.

From beginning to end, Johanna takes us from a never-ending list of things to do all the way to a consistent, understandable mission. Most important, she helps us get to a mission that we can actually accomplish, one where we can be successful.

In my life, I've been successful and I've been unsuccessful, and I like being successful a lot better. If you also prefer to be successful, then Johanna's book can help you. Read it, and try what Johanna suggests. You'll be glad you did.

Ron Jeffries
www.XProgramming.com
www.XProgramming.com/blog

Foreword by Tim Lister

I am writing this in June 2009, and we are currently living in interesting times. These interesting times are demanding that we step up from project management to projects management, and the book in your hand, *Manage Your Project Portfolio*, is going to help you do just that.

There are plenty of good resources on project management that will help you run a project efficiently, but darned few help you get the priorities right. We have spent years as managers worrying about getting the process right, and don't get me wrong, the process does matter, but first things first, let's get the valuable projects to the front of the queue. Let's not worry about starting those projects; let's worry about finishing those projects.

With this book Johanna shows that she understands priorities; first be effective, and then worry about efficiency. Effective means that you are investing in the right projects—those with meaningful value and with risk you can deal with. And as Johanna points out, it is not a matter of "commit" or "kill." It can be "transform"—a chance to mold the value and slough off the project fluff. As a manager, the commit-kill-transform debate leads to the most critical set of decisions a project organization can make. Have some beautifully executed projects that deliver marginal value, and you are spiraling down. Have some complex, wild-animal projects that stress the organization but deliver big value to your customers, and you're on the way up.

Setting priorities is hard; it means that not everybody will be thrilled. Some will be downright angry, but setting priorities and then resetting them as the world changes, without being simply reactive to pressure, has a name. It is management. Management is political, in the best Aristotelian sense of the word. Politics is making decisions for the best interests of the community as a whole.

If you can get to a prioritized portfolio of projects, you have made a great step forward, and Johanna urges us to consider an even more difficult change. She wants you to consider making your organization focus on finishing, not starting. She starts Chapter 1 with these three sentences: "Your customers want your products to be filled with great features that are well-tested and run smoothly. They don't care about your projects, and they certainly don't care about your portfolio. Your customers care about your products." Where is the value in a piece of software? It's always in its outputs—what it delivers to the world. The only things that matter are what you deliver to the world. You don't deliver value until you deliver. Somehow we have become a group of starters, not finishers. Many organizations can't seem to say "No" or "Not now" to anybody. They have many understaffed projects crawling along in the name of satisfying all customers. Of course, as Johanna points out, with this "strategy," you are satisfying no customers at all.

This is a book to read in a group, especially if you are starting from scratch, so to speak. This is a book to discuss and debate. It is chock-full of ideas, and it is up to you, the managerial and technical leaders of your organization, to figure out what changes you want to give a concerted effort. To paraphrase the last section of each chapter, now try this book. It's time.

Tim Lister
Principal, The Atlantic Systems Guild, Inc.
New York City

Preface

So many things can bring a project to its knees. Maybe there's too much multitasking. . . or so much technical debt that the project team can't make progress on the current release. . . or so many emergency projects that emergencies have become normal. . . or so many high-priority projects that no one knows which to work on first.

Sure, there are other things that could be a problem: technical staff estimations are way off, your major competitor just released a huge update and your project won't be ready for another six months, the technical challenges of testing (or writing or developing) are more than your testers (or writers or developers) can manage, the project needs more machines or memory or disk drives. . . and the list goes on. But if you dig down far enough, you will often find that multitasking—and its associated issues of emergency projects, technical debt, or people spread across way too many projects—is what has led to most of your problems.

Multitasking occurs when managers don't make decisions about which projects to do first, second, third, last, and, even more important, never. Some managers don't realize it's their job to make those decisions—they think it's their job to try to staff every project. Some managers don't know how to make those decisions. Some management teams can't agree on the decisions. Whatever the reason, when managers don't decide in which order to execute projects and which projects to leave alone, the project teams suffer from multitasking.

Why am I so passionate that you should manage your project portfolio and shouldn't multitask? I fell into managing the project portfolio when I was working at a company that made complex hardware/software systems. I had first been hired as the director of SQA and continuing engineering. Then they decided they needed a program manager to manage the largest program the engineering organization had attempted. I stopped being the director and ran that program.

About four months before our planned release, we had a customer cancel a contract. Management decided to lay off about half the engineering staff. They assigned someone else to manage the program and asked me to be the director of software engineering.

We were down to about thirty to forty people in development. We had to finish the development work on the program and continue to respond to problems in the field. Each field problem was a crisis and required several weeks of work. So here I am a director, with an interim VP, people who'd been working crazy hours for months, and a release we had to get out. And huge problems we had to fix. We had to do it all. We had no choice.

I made a spreadsheet of what everyone was working on so I could understand where the time was going. I'd made spreadsheets like that before when I'd managed testers and developers who were matrixed into projects, but I had never had to staff quite so many simultaneous projects.

After two weeks of people working the way they'd been assigned, I realized no one was making progress on anything. I sat down with the managers who reported to me. We discussed what work we would staff and not staff. We assigned people to no more than two projects in any given week. We made sure people had team members they could work with to finish the work.

I took the heat from senior management—and there was plenty of it. "You have to do this project and that one and that other one and that other one over there. This week."

I said, "Sorry, we can't do that much in one week. You have to choose."

And of course they rebutted with, "No, you have to do it all."

I said, "Well, then I'll choose."

"You'd better be right."

After another two weeks, we started to make progress, but it still wasn't fast enough. I had a team meeting with my managers and asked, "What will it take to finish this project? Just this one here?" One of the managers said, "If Tom and Harry and Jane can concentrate on just that project for a week, we can finish it."

I said, "OK, have them do that. Now, what about that crisis over there?"

"Well, we need Harry...."

"Sorry, you can't have him. Who else can you use, and how long will it take?"

We had that conversation for all the outstanding work. Now we had small teams assigned to a bunch of the problems so we could fix them and get some breathing room. In about a week, we would be half-staffed on the program, and in about two weeks, we would be back to full staffing on the program. The developers were thrilled to finish something. The managers were happy about not having to move people around. I was happy that we finally got some things done. My senior managers were unhappy with my progress.

After two months of this, we finally had just new development to do on the program, because the continuing engineering department was able to keep up with the field problems. That's when we started to make huge progress on the release, because we were working by feature and assessing our progress biweekly.

We used a combination of approaches: continuing engineering used a kanban approach because the problems were smaller than the features for a release. They could limit their work in progress and work on one problem at a time until it was fixed. Development (and the test group) used two-week timeboxes, working in features, so we could finish chunks of work.

By the end of the four months, we had a release, although we didn't have all the features our senior management wanted. We had the field problems under control. We hadn't added a ton of technical debt.

But the people who remained learned that they could work on one project at a time, one task at a time, until it was done. They could make more progress doing one thing at a time than splitting their time among several pieces of work, even if the work was related.

If I could manage the project portfolio with an organization reeling from a layoff, where we had an unstated strategic plan, where the senior managers had trouble deciding what to do on any given day, you can do this for your work. You may need different approaches for different groups. One group might need to limit the work in progress, especially if you're in a serial life cycle and people with different specialties cycle in and out of the project. One group might need to work in one-week or two-week timeboxes, while another might find three-week timeboxes easier to manage.

Here's the secret of project portfolio management: you can do it all. Just not all at the same time.

Whether you're a manager or not, you need to have a view of all the work underway and all the work you want to do. That's the only way you can make good decisions about which projects to do when and with which people. Even if those people are only you.

Effective managers and leaders create and use a pipeline view of all of the projects, those in progress and those desired. They can see all the potential work, as well as the people and other resources available, and then match the work to the company's (or group's) mission and strategic direction. This collection of projects is an essential tool called the *project portfolio*.

Managers who lead make the difficult portfolio decisions. They look at their company's mission, they look at their mission, and they decide. They decide on the mix of projects the technical staff can start at one time, how long they are willing to let those projects run, and when they need results. They decide on the strategically and tactically important work. Then they do it.

Managers who manage the project portfolio decide when they need to review project status. They have criteria by which to decide whether the projects should continue. And if a project is not providing value to the organization and should not continue, these managers kill those projects. These managers learn their technical staff's capacity so they can plan. And, they make all of these difficult decisions that will allow the organization to be successful.

Managers are leaders when they make the portfolio decisions. Managers are leaders when they guide a team to success. Managers are leaders when they request the team commit to finishing a doable amount of work in a reasonable amount of time.

You don't need to be a senior manager to manage the portfolio. Sure, it helps if the organization has a strategy that translates into a mission, which guides the top-level portfolio development down to the bottom-most level. But let's face it, most organizations don't have that.

You need to understand your mission, understand all the missions between you and the top of the organization, and know how to collaborate across the organization. Then you can develop and manage a project portfolio successfully. Once you've defined the project ranking, you communicate that project ranking to the entire organization, staff the highest-ranked projects, and let your staff know which projects they can ignore for now.

You may never have heard of project portfolio management. Or, maybe you've heard of a bunch of mathematical formulas that even if you can understand, you'll never get your peers or managers to understand and see. We'll use some measurements, but no math. It's easy to understand, and it will help you make decisions. But the hard part of portfolio management is not the math. You may find some of the decisions difficult, but the hard part is sticking with those decisions until it's time to reevaluate the portfolio.

Great managers build trusting relationships with their teams (*Behind Closed Doors* [RD05]). In addition, great managers lead their organizations by selecting the work to do and *not* to do, and therefore they deliver results to the organization and build capacity in their teams. This book is about that kind of leadership.

Before we get started, I thank all the people who took the time to review and help prepare this book. They are Clarke Ching, Linda Cook, Esther Derby, Mark Druy, Mike Dwyer, George Dinwiddie, Don Gray, Ron Jeffries, Andy Hunt, Hannu Kokko, Tim Lister, Hal Macomber, Robert McBride, Steve Peter, Dwayne Phillips, Dave W. Smith, Daniel Steinberg, Dave Thomas, Gerald M. Weinberg, and Kim Wimpsett.

Any remaining mistakes are mine.

If you're ready to lead your team, group, or organization, this book is for you. Let's start.

Johanna Rothman
July 2009

Chapter 1

Meet Your Project Portfolio

Your customers want your products to be filled with great features that are well-tested and run smoothly. They don't care about your projects, and they certainly don't care about your portfolio. Your customers care about your products.

Keep that in mind as you work with your project portfolio. The portfolio is not an end—it's a means. Think of your portfolio as a pipeline of potential work.

You will use your project portfolio to help you make the right decisions to release valuable products frequently enough to fulfill your customers' needs. The best way to do this is to use a lean and agile approach to your projects and to your project portfolio.

In this chapter I'll introduce you to what a project portfolio might look like for you at your level of influence and for your kinds of projects. In a way, that's like saying I'll introduce you to your appointment calendar. You don't value an appointment calendar or a project portfolio until you start using it to shape your days, weeks, and months. That's the job of the rest of the book.

In the following chapters you'll learn how to create, evaluate, rank the contents of, collaborate on, iterate on, evolve, and measure your project portfolio.

You'll follow this flow:

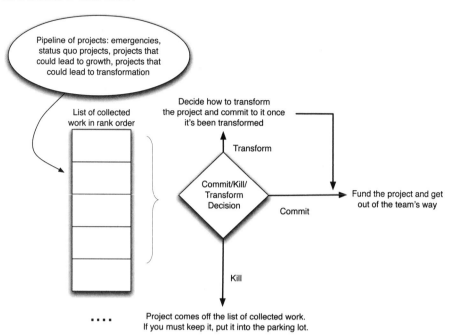

You collect all the work from the pipeline of projects and rank it. Then, make the commit to/kill/transform decision so you can provide maximum value to the organization. Repeat as often as you decide you need to make the project portfolio decision.

1.1 What a Project Portfolio Is

The portfolio is an organization of projects, by date and value, that the organization commits to or is planning to commit to. In a sense, the portfolio is a Big Visible Chart.

It will help you decide the following:

- When to commit to a project so a product development team can start or continue a project.
- When it's time to end a project and free a team for other work.
- When to transform a project and commit to the changed project.
- And, when it's difficult to decide between projects, the portfolio provides a visual tool that helps you negotiate which project to do when.

Agile Approaches Help Project Portfolio Management

If everyone in your organization (senior managers, middle managers, technical leads, functional managers, and project managers) is wedded to a serial life cycle and no one is willing to consider finishing valuable chunks of work frequently, you can't use a pragmatic approach to managing the project portfolio. But if you're willing to consider frequent releases of running, tested features as in *Extreme Programming Installed* (JAH02), you can be successful.

If you're already using an agile approach for your projects or an iterative or incremental life cycle where you have an opportunity before the end of the project to finish features, you can use the ideas here to be a successful leader in the organization, no matter what level you are.

If you use a serial life cycle where you can't see any progress until the end of a project, you will find these ideas more difficult to use. If you use a serial life cycle, try to create interim deliverables. The more frequently the projects deliver something you can see, the easier it will be to manage the project and to manage the project portfolio.

You'll keep all of the work in progress and all of the planned work in your project portfolio. This is not a static document or useless artifact. This is a tool the product development teams and managers use to make the necessary trade-offs of which work to start and finish now, what to do later, and what to do never.

The teams use the portfolio to see which projects to spend time on now and what they might do in the future. Most important, they know where *not* to spend their time. The managers use the portfolio to make sure the organization is working on the most valuable work—the strategically important work.

Those product development teams may have any number of names: IT, R&D, engineering, or even something else. The name doesn't matter. What matters is that there are knowledge workers available to the organization to innovate, to create, and to develop the products the organizations uses or sells to improve its business.

The portfolio is the closest thing to the product development organization's backlog, because it's organized by priority. But the portfolio also provides you with a picture of the projects over time, so you can manage project interactions, who's assigned to which projects, and the general risk and value of each project.

Managing the project portfolio is context-dependent. Your project life cycles, your budgeting process, and how you do road maps all affect the project portfolio.

If you're willing to adopt lean concepts, you'll find it easy to manage the portfolio. These ideas include eliminating waste as you work your way through projects; discovering and eliminating roadblocks to throughput; evening the workload for people and teams; optimizing for the entire organization, not just one piece of it; completing valuable features in short time periods; and not creating inventory of partially completed work.

1.2 See the High- and Low-Level Views

Just as you want to see your calendar in high-level views (yearly and monthly) and in more detailed views (weekly and daily), you'll need to look at your portfolio the same way. Sometimes, you need to see the big picture for the whole organization to see where people are working. Sometimes, you need to see the details to understand who is doing what and when.

Throughout this book we'll look at a variety of tools for working with the information you store in your portfolio. You often have to decide whether you need to take a high-level look at your portfolio to get a feel for all of the projects you have working or a low-level view that shows you more of the details but less of the overall pattern.

The following is a high-level picture of the portfolio for the organization. You can see when the projects start and when everyone *expects* them to finish. This portfolio is at too high a level to see who's doing what. But, if you are looking at the chart in January, you can see which projects have actually started, which ones you want to start (Project3), and which ones are scheduled to start.

Month/Projects	January	February	March	April	May
	Project1	Project1	Project1		
	Project2	Project2	Project2		
Unstaffed Work		Project3	Project3	Project3	
			Project4	Project4	Project4
				Project5	Project5

I like using "unstaffed" for projects that haven't started yet or for ones I wish I could start but don't have the staff to start yet. That's because I want to know the following:

- Have we started to work on this project at all? If so, can the project team measure its velocity and use that as a prediction when we'll be done enough with this project?

- Do we need to reevaluate the portfolio if we have not yet started this project?

- Based on changing market or business needs, do we need to change who is assigned to the project, whether we should staff this project, or whether we should change the project?

Answering yes to any of these questions means it's time to rethink your management decisions about projects.

If you use an agile life cycle, see how your portfolio might look, especially if you have to support already-existing projects:

Week Team	Week 1	Week 2	Week 3	Week 4	Week 5
Tina, Tristan, Isabel, Inge, Sebastian	Project 1	Project 1	Support Work	Project 1	Project 1
Irene, Stuart, Steve, Sandy, Betty, Brian	Project 2	Project 2	Support Work	Project 4	Project 4
Unstaffed work	Project 3	Project 3	Project 3	Project 3	Project 3

In this portfolio, you can see that the teams work on one project for a two-week timebox, do a week of support, and then work on a project for another two-week timebox.[1] This is not the only way to manage support work, but the portfolio makes that decision transparent.

This next figure is another view of a low-level portfolio, where you can see who is assigned to which projects and, in this case, features for the projects.

This organization is using an incremental life cycle, not an agile life cycle.

	Week1	Week2	Week3	Week4
Tina	Project1 Feature 1	Project1 Feature 1	Project1 Feature 4	Project1 Feature 4
Terri	Project1 Feature 1	Project1 Feature 1	Project1 Feature 4	Project1 Feature 4
Tristan	Project1 Feature 2	Project1 Feature 2	Project1 Feature 5	Project 2 Feature 1
Isabel	Project1 Feature 2	Project1 Feature 2	Project1 Feature 5	Project 2 Feature 1
Irene	Project 3 Feature 17	Project 3 Feature 17	Project 3 Feature 17	Project 2 Feature 1
Inge	Project 3 Feature 17	Project 3 Feature 17	Project 3 Feature 17	Project 1 Feature 7
Stuart	Project 3 Feature 17	Project 3 Feature 17	Project 3 Feature 17	Project 1 Feature 7
Steve	Project 1 Feature 3	Project 1 Feature 3	Project1 Feature 6	Project 1 Feature 7
Sandy	Project 1 Feature 3	Project 1 Feature 3	Project1 Feature 6	Project 1 Feature 7
Betty	Project 1 Feature 3	Project 1 Feature 3	Project1 Feature 6	Project 1 Feature 7
Brian	Project 1 Feature 3	Project 1 Feature 3	Project1 Feature 6	Project 1 Feature 7
Mary Man	Management	Management	Management	Management
Unstaffed work				
	Project 3, Feature 18	Project 3, Feature 18	Project 3, Feature 18	Project 2, Features 2, 3, 4
				Project 3, Feature 18

This portfolio reflects who's working on which feature in an incremental life cycle. It's clear who is assigned to which feature and what work this group cannot start until some people finish what they are doing—or until someone in management changes the priority of the work.

Connecting Management's Desires with Reality
by Vijay, Development Manager/Project Manager

My manager came to me with yet another project. So, I showed him my monthlong project portfolio, with all the unstaffed work. He said, "But we want these three projects done," as he pointed to the high-level portfolio. I swallowed and said, "Well, we can't do them in this time with the other work we have."

He sighed. With the evidence in front of him, in a picture with colors, he couldn't argue. Well, he could, but it wouldn't have helped. I said, "Look, we can work in shorter timeboxes. We can start—and finish—fewer

---

1. Notice that all of these portfolio pictures start and end neatly on month or week boundaries. That's not because portfolios work like that but because it's easier to show the month or week boundary in a picture. If you finish a project or a feature on a Wednesday, your next project or feature would start on Thursday.

features. You could even give me more open reqs so I can hire more people. I guess we could incur some technical debt, but that would anger Major Big Customer. Have you really ranked the projects in the order you want them? If you have, we need magic. But maybe you can rerank and have *everyone* in the group work on just one project. We could finish that one and then go on to the next one.

Having the high-level perspective helps the whole organization see what the company expects each group to do. Having the low-level perspective helps the project team and first-level managers make the current reality match expectations.

There is nothing like showing your manager data to help set their expectations about what you can—and cannot—do.

1.3 Now Try This

- Are you concerned about using a portfolio to organize your projects? If so, write down why you're concerned. Keep that list in front of you as you read this book, so you can address your concerns.

- Is there any reason you would not want the transparency a project portfolio provides you? Keep those reasons in mind as you read the next chapter.

- If you work on projects with a serial life cycle, see whether there are natural completion points where you can assess the project state for the purposes of a project portfolio.

Chapter 2

See Your Future

Portfolios do one thing extremely well: they make the organization's choices crystal clear. In this chapter, we'll look at what your life might look like when you decide to change how you manage.

2.1 Managing with a Project Portfolio

Portfolios make choices clear because they help leaders restrict which work the project staff starts and finishes. If you use project portfolios, you have the maximum flexibility as a manager. But if you've never seen a portfolio or you've never used one, you might be concerned, as one of my colleagues explained, "But, JR, if I commit to a project portfolio, I won't have the flexibility I need to manage what my group does when. I can't be responsive to the needs of the organization. I won't be a team player."

A portfolio can help you be responsive, especially when project teams work feature by feature in short time periods. When you manage the portfolio, you limit the number of active projects. The fewer number of active projects you have, the less competition the projects have for the same people. That lack of competition for people allows them to finish projects faster. You increase the number of completed projects, which reduces the total number of projects the organization needs to manage and allows new projects to start. That makes it easier to manage the portfolio. Managing the portfolio increases your organization's throughput.

The cause and effects of managing the project portfolio are shown in Figure 2.1, on the following page. You'll still have difficult decisions to make. You may not know if your mission needs to change. You may

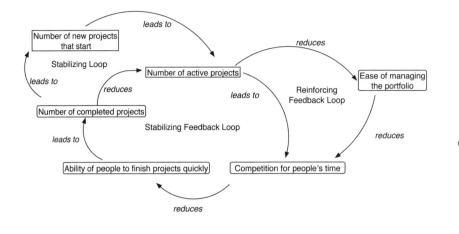

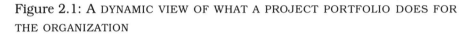

Figure 2.1: A DYNAMIC VIEW OF WHAT A PROJECT PORTFOLIO DOES FOR
THE ORGANIZATION

have loud discussions about which project really is number one. And,
as you work through those decisions, you'll discover that you are per-
forming the difficult work of leading the organization by deciding what
to do now, what to do later, and what not to do.

When you live with a project portfolio, the portfolio allows you to create
a master plan. It creates a transparent link from the projects with their
schedules and iterations to the portfolio.

2.2 Managing Without a Project Portfolio

Managing without a project portfolio leaves you and everyone around
you with all sorts of debt.

When you don't manage the project portfolio, you incur management
debt by having to make more and more critical decisions without sufficient data. The products incur technical debt in the form of people
taking shortcuts to complete projects because they have too much to
work on to take the time to do whatever they need to do right. And as
an organization, you incur capability debt, because people (managers
and technical staff) can't improve their capabilities when they're overburdened with too much work to do. Without a portfolio, your situation
looks something like Figure 2.2.

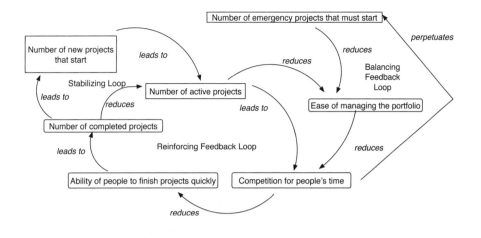

Figure 2.2: A DYNAMIC VIEW OF WHAT HAPPENS WHEN NO ONE MANAGES THE PROJECT PORTFOLIO

When your organization's management refuses to make a project portfolio, that lack of decision making is guaranteeing at least one or more schedule games (see *Manage It!* [Rot07]). Or, people will decide which project to work on first, and that decision may not agree with yours. Without project portfolio management, you have more projects competing for the same—and limited—number of people. You find you can't commit to which people work on which projects when, you're awash in emergency projects, and you and your staff are running yourselves ragged multitasking.[1]

When you don't manage the project portfolio, you prevent the people from finishing projects quickly. You have more and more unfinished projects and fewer completed projects. That increases the number of projects you have. And, the more projects you have competing for the same staff, the more disorganized and split you become, and the more emergencies you generate for overlooked and neglected projects (like the ones you or your manager forgot about until they became emergencies). All this increases organizational complexity and makes it harder to manage the portfolio and, even worse, to finish anything of value for the organization.

---

1. These can be seen in the Split Focus or Pants on Fire schedule games.

The lack of decision making at the top flows down to lower-level managers and technical leads. It's tough to be a senior manager. If you're in a tight financial situation, making the wrong decision can make things much worse. I've worked with senior managers who were paralyzed by the fear of not making enough money, not having the right mix of products, or some other issue. They literally could not decide how to rank the project priorities in a portfolio. If you're in that position, start at Section 11.8, *How to Define a Mission When No One Else Will*, on page 156. The mission will help guide your decisions. An agile approach to your projects allows you to take on risky projects, by helping you manage the risk, as in Section 5.4, *Rank the Projects by Risk*, on page 55.

If you're a first-level or middle manager, it's possible your management hasn't decided on a corporate strategy. If that's true, you can use your portfolio to help them decide by defining your mission along with your portfolio. See Chapter 11, *Define Your Mission*, on page 147.

Whatever you do, don't hide from ranking the projects in your portfolio. When you or your manager refuses to make a project portfolio, your lack of decision making is guaranteeing at least one or more schedule games (see *Manage It!* [Rot07]). Or, people will decide which project to work on first—and that decision may not agree with yours. Look at the feedback loop in Figure 2.1, on page 10.

If you don't decide which project is first, second, and third, you encourage people to work on zero projects.

A Tale of Three Projects
by Aiden, Hapless Developer

I'm sitting at my desk, completely stuck. I have three must-finish-now, ultra-high crisis projects. Every time I start one, someone interrupts me with a question on one of the others. I can't escape anywhere—people have found me in the cafeteria, in the meeting room, in the lab. My manager came by yesterday morning to tell me the first project needs to be done now. Then he came by after lunch to tell me the second project needs to be done now. I stopped working on the first and started on the second. Then he told me at the end of the day that I need to finish the third.

I can't decide what to do first. What's the point of working on any one of these projects? He'll just come by and tell me to change before I finish anything. Maybe I'll work on my resume or play a game of solitaire.

You want people excited about working for your company. That's part of creating a great work environment. Continuous multitasking doesn't just prevent people from accomplishing work; it also creates low morale. Managing the project portfolio isn't easy. But it's necessary.

Everyone, no matter where you are in the organization, needs to know enough about portfolios to collect their work, to organize their work, to help evaluate each piece of work against the other work, and to be able to say no to more work.

2.3 What Are Your Emergency Projects?

When I was developing the feedback loops (in Figure 2.2, on page 11) so you could see the difference between managing the portfolio and not managing the portfolio, I was explaining to a colleague what I meant by emergency projects—those projects that start because of technical debt. But my colleague asked, "What if the world changes and you need to change everything you do?"

When the world changes, you may have to throw out most of your projects and start all over again. That's because of disruptive change. Highsmith discussed this in *Adaptive Software Development* [Hig99] as early as 1999. That's why you need your mission. With a mission, you can update your strategy and tactics (which projects to do when) so you can respond to disruptive change without going out of business. Sure, you might have to change your mission or strategy, but if you don't know where you are, you can't go someplace else.

But emergency projects that arise from technical debt don't occur with disruptive change. Emergency projects exist to satisfy a customer who's not getting what he or she wants, e.g., a lack of features, too many defects or other obvious technical debt, a project that was later than desired. If you don't rank the backlog, you might be missing a feature when you need it. If you don't check the design as you implement features, the next feature may not fit into the system. If you don't write the code, you certainly won't have the feature. If you don't test the product well enough, some features might not work or might not work in tandem in the system. Emergency projects are the result of technical debt and managerial debt.

If you're collecting all the work and actively managing the portfolio by reviewing it frequently enough, you rarely have emergency projects. That's because you see little problems before they become big problems; because you see progress or lack of it in a project; and because project teams rarely incur technical debt because you're using the measure of running, tested features to manage the portfolio. And, if the world changes, you're reviewing the portfolio often enough that you can choose to commit to different projects if the world shifts.

2.4 Lean Approaches to the Project Portfolio

I've said you need to consider lean and agile approaches to your projects and the portfolio. Agile thinking is the frequent—no more than four weeks—release of valuable chunks of product. If you're not familiar with lean, consider some of the principles of lean in *Lean Thinking* [WJ96], *Lean Product and Process Development* [War07], and *The Toyota Way* [Lik04]:

- Think in terms of value. Producers create value, but customers define it.

- Know how you create value. The value stream is how you identify the problem you want to solve, how you manage creating the solution to that problem, and how the customer acquires the solution.

- Create process flow to make problems more transparent. The team has what they need (people, knowledge, material, whatever) to work in small chunks that they can handle and complete. When a problem arises, they fix it.

- Use pull systems to avoid overproduction. Instead of creating "inventory," you create just the piece of the product you need now. For those of you who are accustomed to attempting to define all the requirements up front, you instead define the most valuable requirement, and the team implements that. You avoid all the work of gathering and defining requirements that are wrong, as well as the work to implement them.

- Level out the workload. Make sure people finish the work already in process before they start on new work. That eliminates multitasking.

- Stop when there is a quality problem. If you work in small, doable chunks and you finish one chunk before starting a new one, you will immediately know whether there is a quality problem. If there is, you fix it before going on to another task.

- Use visual control so no problems are hidden. Information radiators such as velocity charts, burndown or burnup charts, and the project portfolio backlog burndown charts make the state clear to everyone.

If you keep these approaches in mind as you create and manage the project portfolio, you'll discover you can shift your focus from math based on prediction to collaboration with others in the organization.[2]

2.5 Why You Should Care About the Project Portfolio

If you're a senior or middle manager, you care about the project portfolio, because that's how you predict whether the organization can get enough value out of its projects to remain on track—or, even better, to grow. The more projects your organization can complete, the more value you can realize from the work (assuming you're evaluating the projects in a way that makes sense), and the more value *you* provide to the larger organization.

As a middle manager, you are trying to finish and then start more projects. Without real data about project progress, or without the ability to make a reasonable prediction of how long a project might take, you can't be successful with all of your responsibilities.

As a technical lead or first-level manager, you care about finishing projects, but you likely have a more immediate problem—how to get enough people to finish the projects your management wants you to finish. The portfolio helps you show your managers when you need more people and what types of people they are.

2.5.1 Why Technical Leads Care About Portfolio Management

If you're a technical lead, do you still need to care about the project portfolio? Yes. If you have responsibility for a product, you are a technical lead and need to make sure you and your team are working on the highest-value work and that your work is transparent to the rest of the organization.

---

2.   Another idea that's key to learn is continuous improvement. You'll see throughout this book that your portfolio is not a static document. You will continue to work to improve it to meet your current needs.

Do You Always Need to Manage the Project Portfolio?

A senior manager asked me, "Hey, life is good. We're making money hand over fist. Why do we need to keep managing the portfolio?"

In a great economy, you don't have enough people for all the projects you want to do. So, ranking the projects by value and making sure you finish the most valuable projects buys you enough time and money to find the people to do the work and to keep you profitable.

A down economy is the ideal time to choose the projects with the highest value to the organization. This keeps the organization going through the hard times. And, in a really tough economy, you need the portfolio with a lean and agile approach to take on the risky projects that might make the difference between your organization thriving and going under.

If you can predict the future, quit your management job, and make a killing on the stock market. But if you're like the rest of us, you'll need to keep evaluating and reviewing the portfolio so you can deliver the highest value to the organization. It's a tough job, and you'll be great at it.

Keeping Up with All My Projects
by John, Technical Lead

I haven't been here long, but I've already accumulated projects that only *I* have worked on. One of the projects encompasses the financial reports for the CFO out of our site. It was supposed to be a short, small project two years ago. It was, then. Since then, I've added at least twenty new features and fixed a bunch of cosmetic problems.

It's not hard work, but every time I got heads-down on something else, the CFO called my manager and asked me to do something else. I finally got tired of it and created a portfolio for my boss and me and a product backlog for the CFO. Now when he calls, I can show my manager what I'm doing, and we can schedule his changes in a way that make sense for everyone.

Sure, I had to do a quick fix last week when we got a new request from our auditors. That was an interruption—it didn't go on the backlog. But that's just one problem out of the last few where I've had to interrupt myself. The portfolio helps me organize my work. And, the backlog helps my customers know when I'll get to their problem and in which order.

> **Managing the Project Portfolio Reduces Schedule Games**
>
> Until you set your priorities, you are susceptible to various schedule games. If you can't decide which project is the number-one project for you or your team to work on, you might be suffering from the Pants on Fire schedule game. Or, if you are attempting to work on more than one project at a time, you are suffering from the Split Focus schedule game.
>
> If you have a project portfolio where the organization's priorities are set, these schedule games become irrelevant, you get more work done, and you finish more projects.

Project portfolios make your work visible. Without them, no one realizes all the little pieces of work you're doing. You have to make that visible, and a portfolio is an ideal tool.

2.5.2 Why Some Managers Don't Like Project Portfolios

Some managers are concerned that project portfolios restrict their options. They do. You are committed to honor these restrictions until the next time you evaluate the portfolio. Several managers have said, "But I won't get to move people around day by day to where I need them." Exactly. I assume you want your staff to complete projects. Moving people around frequently—and incurring the costs of multitasking—is the wrong action. The books *Quality Software Management: Volume 1, Systems Thinking* [Wei92]; *Slack: Getting Past Burnout, Busywork, and the Myth of Total Efficiency* [DeM01]; and *Multiprojecting: The Illusion of Progress* [Rot04b] all discuss this. To see a collection of articles that discuss the costs of multitasking, see http://www.umich.edu/~bcalab/multitasking.html.

Project portfolios don't restrict your options as a manager. In fact, if you use a project portfolio, you will find you have more choices of when to start and finish which work, assuming you use lean and agile approaches to your product development; see Chapter 9, *Evolve Your Portfolio*, on page 113.

> ### Avoid Using the Portfolio as Wishful Artifact
>
> A colleague told me about their project portfolio. "We plan and faithfully reevaluate the project portfolio every quarter. We make a nice spreadsheet. And then, the next day—or at least the next week—we change who's working on what. Our portfolios look like our project Gantt charts: they look nice until reality sets in, and then the next day or week they are wrong."
>
> Although the portfolio is a living document, if you change your mind more often than you change the portfolio, you're wasting your time attempting to rank the portfolio and explain what people need to work on and not work on.
>
> The project portfolio is most valuable when the decision makers agree that for the next month (or two or three) the technical staff will work on these projects in this order. Then the technical staff do the work. At the end of the evaluation period, the decision makers decide the ranking for the next period.

2.6 Your Portfolio Reflects Your Influence Level

Your portfolio will reflect the work you influence. Without regard to your title, consider the level at which you work. That level depends on how much of a product you can produce by yourself and who makes the decision about who to assign to projects when.

Your level	How you make portfolio decisions
First-level manager	Your boss tells you which projects to do when. You might make the decision jointly with your boss. You do not interact with your peers or with senior managers.
Middle manager	You decide which projects to do when, possibly with your boss' input. Your boss or a senior management committee has the final decision.
Senior manager	You make all the project portfolio decisions independently, or with a peer group of senior managers who can commit the organization to work.

Even if you produce a whole product, as in the case of an agile team or even a program of agile teams, but you don't have the ability to determine which project is number one, you're a first-level manager for the purposes of the project portfolio.

> **┊/╱ Joe Asks...**
> **╰ᵕ╯ What If My Organization Doesn't Want to Change?**
>
> Change what you can.
>
> Throughout this book I talk about making decisions for you, your team, and your organization based on business value. Your reality may make this difficult. Even if you don't get buy-in or support from above, you can still benefit from creating and managing a project portfolio. It will provide the support and stability your team needs. Your portfolio will help you answer your managers' questions more quickly and completely—even if they don't buy into the notion of portfolios.

As you read this book, think about your level so you can make the best decisions in your sphere of influence.

2.7 Now Try This

- Do you know the cost of multitasking in your organization? If not, ask everyone in your group to track their time for no more than one week. Ask each person to count the number of times they multitask during the day. Ask them to estimate how long it took to move away from the first task to the second one and how long it took to reenter the context of the original task. You will be dismayed. Determine an average cost per day of multitasking.

- If your manager thinks this is a bunch of hooey, walk him or her through the cause-and-effect diagrams. Then discuss what multitasking is costing your department.

- Track the number of emergency projects you have to see whether you are falling into the traps of working with no portfolio.

- If you've been managing your own project portfolio for a while, this part may seem like a review for you. In that case, consider how you'll help your peers collect their work and how you'll work together to evaluate, rank, and collaborate on the portfolio, especially over time.

Chapter 3

Create the First Draft of Your Portfolio

Now that you understand the basics, it's time to collect all the work you and your group are supposed to be doing. It's easy to get caught up in evaluating the work while you are collecting it. Don't. First, make sure you know about all the work people across the organization expect of you. Then and only then will you be able to assign the work to your portfolio by evaluating it and determining whether you need to do it now. Don't try to do everything at once; start collecting all the work before you attempt to evaluate it.

3.1 Know What Work to Collect

You can collect work only in your immediate sphere of influence. That's because you don't know what people two levels up or down from you are actually doing. If you're a first-level manager, you can ask each person in your group what they are working on. But the more middle- or senior-level management you are, the more you have to work through your staff. Explain what you want to know and how you want to see it. You might even use the next few paragraphs to help them understand. Don't be afraid to depend on others to help collect the work; be clear on what you want to see.

As you collect your work or as you ask others to collect theirs, remember to look at all five categories of work—periodic work, ongoing work, emergency work, management work, and project work—to see who's doing what in your portfolio, as in *Behind Closed Doors: Secrets of Great Management* [RD05]. Although you might think of project work first, remember all the other work, too.

Some of your work is organized by time:

- Periodic work, such as monthly reports or yearly budgets or training or vacation. If it's something you need to do at a specific time but is not part of a project, it's periodic work.

- Ongoing work, such as support for the operation of an organization or department. You might need to check on the status of a product owner building a product backlog. You might not want to make this periodic (every Tuesday at 11 a.m.), but you don't want to forget it.

- In-process ad hoc work, such as emergency projects, work you are doing as the result of crises, or other surprises.

In addition, you have work organized by intent:

- Management work, such as meetings with your managers, peers, or staff; strategic planning; coaching; feedback; coordinating the work of other people—anything that helps you make a decision about who should do what and when. You don't need to be a manager to perform "management" work.

- Project work, such as the project to save the company, a hotfix, or work to determine whether you want to acquire another organization. Projects are not limited to technical staff. A project has a specific objective and a projected end date.

Once you gather all the work, you can organize it week by week and person by person so you can see what's really going on.

One way to do this is to make a chart like this:

Tasks	Week 1	Week 2	Week 3	Week 4
Unstaffed work				

Make a yellow sticky of each piece of work you are supposed to do. If you are working on a project for several weeks, make a sticky for that project for each week. Put all the stickies in the appropriate week, above the "Unstaffed work" line. Just get them all in.

If you're a middle or senior manager, ask the managers who work for you to do this with their groups also. I suggest you start this as a person-by-person bottom-up activity so you can see what each person in the organization is doing and planning to do for the next few weeks. This will provide you with an early warning of multitasking or emergency projects. When you start with the projects and work down, people sometimes forget all the other little pieces of work, and it's more difficult to see the multitasking.

If you are working on just one project, especially if your project is using timeboxes of up to four weeks and you work feature by feature so you finish valuable work at the end of each timebox, this is a trivial step. However, even if you're working in an agile way or if you're working on several projects, collect all your work anyway. You need to see what other people expect of you.

> ### Turn Ongoing Work into Periodic Work
>
> I admit it, I forget things unless I've written them down. I'm especially bad with ongoing work, which is why I like to turn ongoing work into periodic work as quickly as possible.
>
> If you know you need to check on something, schedule it as a periodic to-do in your calendar, on the same day of the week and at the same time, and make it a repeating task. When I'm a manager, I do this with one-on-ones. When I'm a project manager, I turn my informal check-withs into repeating tasks. A check-with is "Check with Ted to see whether he's updating the backlog for the next iteration's planning." If you realize you don't need to do this task this week, that's great. You've freed yourself from a task. If you don't need to do it three times in a row, maybe you don't need to do it at all. Or, maybe you change the periodicity of it.

Now, be honest with yourself, and put the work you can't do in a given week into the unstaffed work row. Now you have something to discuss with your manager or your customers. You may have to say no to some work, as in Section 6.6, *How to Say No to More Work*, on page 76.

3.2 Is the Work a Project or a Program?

I meet lots of technical leads, project managers, and functional managers who claim to be working on seven, eight, nine, ten, twenty, and forty-seven projects. No one can manage that many projects. When I ask more questions, I discover I can clump the projects into these categories:

- Large projects that keep evolving because the project team is not working feature by feature in timeboxed iterations. Because it's not clear when the project will be done, people across the organization request more and more features, resulting in the "never-ending project." The project is valuable to the organization; it's just not clear if or when it will ever be done.

- Small projects that are unique and that result in a particular valuable deliverable.

- Small pieces that are needed for a single deliverable but have limited use by themselves. These projects are part of a program and need a program manager.

- Large projects that aren't due *yet* but will be an emergency when they are due if the project teams don't start on them. Because they aren't due yet and the project managers and the teams have so much to do, they postpone working on these projects until they are an emergency.

In your portfolio, you want to manage the different kinds of work differently. Any project that has a valuable deliverable, whether it's small or large, needs to be in your portfolio, with a unique team and due date associated with it. But those small pieces of projects—those are not projects per se.

If you have a collection or series of small pieces that individually don't add up to significant value—but *together* do create substantial value, consider collecting them as a program. Then you add that program to your project portfolio.

3.3 Organize Your Projects into Programs As Necessary

As you collect the work, especially if you have many projects, think about how to organize the projects.

Are some of the programs from several subprojects? Do some programs have phased releases? Do some products need to be separated into smaller salable or releasable products?

A program is a collection of projects that all together deliver significant value. Each project may have some value by itself. But the real value is the collection of projects into one deliverable: a program. You might have a program of a number of subprojects all with one release date. Or, you might have a program of phased work, where each phase delivers some significant value.

Many of My Projects Are One Program
by Pam, IT Project Manager

I was trying to manage about twenty-five projects. I was going nuts.

Then I realized we didn't have a system unless all twenty-five projects were done. Our system was a program. Even though all my projects were subprojects, I could work with the business to define when the business side wanted to see which feature.

That meant I didn't have to manage each project separately; I had a context for all of them. I could sequence them and still provide a status report for my managers. And, if they canceled the system, I didn't have to keep managing all of those projects.

Now it made sense for me to make sure I had people assigned just to the subprojects we needed done now, not the ones that could wait.

Programs can take several shapes. Be ready to organize the projects into programs where several projects have one interdependent goal, whether that goal is one release, phases of releases, or several products.

3.3.1 Organize Projects into Programs

You might work in an organization that needs program management but doesn't realize it. Here's a simple test. Do you work in an organization where Joe has one project, Sally has another, and Tim has a third but none of them can release their project until all of the projects are ready? If you have interdependencies between projects, you need program management.

Program management can take several forms, but a common form is the mechanism of organizing several interdependent projects together as one program so that the program manager and project managers can manage the interdependencies and successfully release the product. Here Joe, Sally, and Tim all need to complete their projects so that the program can release at one time:

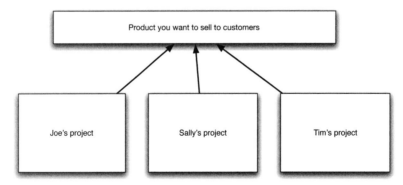

If you're a project manager, your management may not realize they've created a program when they initiated Joe's, Sally's, and Tim's projects. As you collect the work, talk with Joe, Sally, and Tim to see whether they should be working as a program team. If so, it's time to help your colleagues realize the program is one entry in the portfolio, not three entries as separate projects. If you're a middle or senior manager, assign a program manager to bring interdependent projects together.

3.3.2 Organizing Projects into a Phased Program

Another form of a program is a phased series of projects for one product. Sometimes, Joe, Sally, and Tom are working on "independent" projects because they are phased development. That is, Joe's project is responsible for a feature set. Sally and Tom are working on "independent" feature sets—independent as far as what the customer sees. This looks complex, because it *is* complex. It's also much harder to manage a phased program and to make portfolio decisions about it.

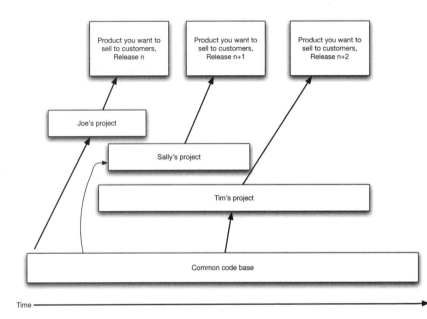

If the projects access the same code base, the projects are *not* independent. The work may be sufficiently long or challenging that you want the projects working at the same time. They are another kind of a program: a phased program where you have release 1, followed by release 2, followed by release 3, and so on. You might need to start working on follow-on releases (which your management thinks are projects) in order to complete them by a desired release date. But those projects are interdependent and need to be managed that way.

You especially want to avoid the situation that release 1 has been released, the market changes, release 2's goals are completely changed, but release 3 doesn't change. If you manage the projects as a phased program, you will at least ask whether release 3's goals should be changed—or even whether you should continue with this project (see Section 4.1, *Should We Do This Project at All?*, on page 33).

Part of the problem with a phased program is that you want to understand how much planning went into these phases. In a number of agile environments, you might see five levels of planning:

- Product vision: A long-term guiding vision for the entire product created by the product owner and/or product manager.
- Product road map: A time-based view of high-level features that the product owner and product manager may want in the product.
- Release plan: For a given release, which of those features the product owner wants the team to deliver.
- Iteration plan: For a specific iteration, what the team commits to deliver.
- Daily commitment: For a specific day, what the team commits to do.

Phased programs occur when one team cannot—by themselves—deliver on the product road map via a release plan in the time the organization wants the features.

3.3.3 Creating One or Several Products

Imagine that you start and complete a project with a limited scope. You add more scope over several releases and some time and realize that this one product actually should be several products.

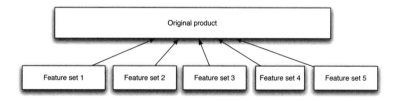

The problem is that you're organized as a massive project or as a program. What can you do?

First, if you're the first-level manager, create a picture of how all the pieces do something different and how they are connected—or not. If you're a higher-level manager, ask the project or program manager to create this picture. This picture helps your peers and managers see when and how to make a decision about several projects or one product and how to organize it.

You might decide to organize it like this:

More likely, you will need some phases to separate the products and to help the customers move.

As you collect the work, keep thinking about how the products or systems work together.

3.4 Organize the Portfolio

When it's time to organize the portfolio from the work, organize it so you can see the timeline of the work moving in one direction (I like left to right) and can see the work from top to bottom, in rank-order priority. If you don't know the rank order now, guess. You can see several approaches to evaluate the portfolio in Chapter 5, *Rank the Portfolio*, on page 47. Use a simple template to help you organize the work.

This starting point doesn't need to be fancy. You are just capturing information. Don't become involved in the formatting and making things look pretty. You can start with something as bare bones as this:

Who	Week 1	Week 2	Week 3	Week 4
Name the person	Describe the work	...		
Name the person	...			
Name the person				
...				
Unstaffed Work				

Notice a few things about the blank portfolio. Since we're starting from gathering the work, the time frame is only a few weeks in duration. You can't predict further out than that, so don't waste your time trying. If you have more than four weeks of work to put in a portfolio, extend the date to the right, and put the work you're *planning* to do in the "Unstaffed Work" area. Yes, I know you (or your group) are planning to do it. But unless you can guarantee yourself that you (or whomever is assigned) is definitely going to do that work at that time, such as a vacation or some external date-driven event like a conference, it's unstaffed work.

If you're working with a group of people to organize the portfolio, have them write their work on stickies or index cards. You can write the blank template on a whiteboard or flip chart, and everyone can post their stickies on the template. You want to end up with a portfolio that could look something like this:

Week Team	Iteration 1	Iteration 1	Iteration 2	Iteration 2	July	August	Sept
Tina, Tristan, Isabel, Inge, Sebastian	Project 1	Project 1	Project 1	Project 1	Project 1 and several vacation weeks	Some vacations and some user group meeting prep	Project 1
Irene, Stuart, Steve, Sandy, Betty, Brian	Project 2	Project 2	Project 4	Project 4	Project 4 and several vacation weeks	some vacations and User group meeting prep	User group meeting
Unstaffed work	Project 3	Project 3	Project 3	Project 3	User group meeting demo, tutorial	User group meeting demo, tutorial	not clear!

This sample portfolio has a clear perspective on the next four weeks and a high-level perspective for another three months, so you can see the user group meeting demo and tutorial work are at risk. Given the unstaffed work, it's not clear what the teams will be doing past June.

3.5 Using Tools to Manage a Portfolio

When I work with managers and management teams, they always want to know what tools they should use to manage the portfolio. When you start with portfolio management, start with stickies on the wall. As you

\\// Joe Asks...
2f

How Do I Create a Portfolio with a Geographically Distributed Team?

OK, index cards won't work with a distributed team. If you can't gather the team together in one room to collect all the work the first time, consider using a wiki, a shared spreadsheet, or a shared drawing. Be ready to iterate so you are collecting all the work and people can see it.

become more facile with developing the portfolio and making decisions, decide whether index cards will work better for you. If you have to share information across a number of sites, a spreadsheet might work. Digital pictures always work.

I'm reluctant to use any high-tech tool to manage the portfolio, because any tool can be difficult to use and prevent people from making decisions as frequently as they need. I much prefer stickies and index cards.

Whatever you use, don't use a Gantt chart to manage the portfolio. Yes, the projects may have interdependencies, but the Gantt chart is the wrong tool. Gantts organize tasks in service to *one* deliverable: a particular release of a specific product. Project portfolios, especially if you color code them in some way, help you see interactions *among* projects in service of creating value to the organization.

3.6 Now Try This

- Make yourself a project portfolio template, and post it on your whiteboard or on a flip chart.
- Take ten minutes, and write down everything you're doing on stickies. If you're managing a team of people or several teams or an organization, ask your managers to do this with you. The more people in your organization, the longer this step will take. Timebox it so people aren't staring into space but are writing.
- Post the stickies on the template in the correct weeks.
- Leave the portfolio on your wall for a few days to a week. As you discover other work, make more stickies and post them.

Chapter 4

Evaluate Your Projects

Once you have collected all your work into a draft portfolio, you'll evaluate each project or program. For the purposes of managing the project portfolio, treat your programs and projects in the same way. You don't have to do anything special to evaluate programs.

It's difficult to decide which work is most valuable and which work should be done first, so separate those decisions. The first time you organize your work into a portfolio, you don't have to make the ranking decision. Your very first decision is about whether you *want* to commit to this project, kill the project, or transform the project in some way before continuing.

Resist the temptation to say "I want to do this project first" or third or seventh as you proceed with the initial evaluation. When you separate the evaluation from the ranking, it's easier to make all the decisions. You'll have an opportunity to rank after you evaluate each project or program.

4.1 Should We Do This Project at All?

Before you try to decide where each project fits in the portfolio, ask, "Should we do this project at all?" If the answer is no, take the project off the list. If the answer is yes, select a way or ways to rank order the projects in the portfolio. Take the time to ask this simple question of each and every project in your portfolio.

You may not feel as if you have the right to ask this question. You do.

If you're a first-level manager in terms of influence, you have intimate knowledge of the project and the product it will create or extend. You know about the strategic importance of this project with respect to the product. If you're a middle manager, you can see all the initiatives and can consider the evaluation of this project with respect to the others. If you're a senior manager, you can see the entire organization's strategic direction and see whether this project should be done at all with respect to all the initiatives across the organization.

Any time you have a chance to eliminate a project from consideration, do so. As you review the portfolio over time, note which projects you don't ever give many points. Can you take those projects off the list altogether? If not, can you create a small project or a short iteration to provide you with some information about whether this project is worth the aggravation of considering?

Sometimes, you'll put projects into the portfolio and not get to them for a while. Sometimes a very long while. If that's the case with some of your projects, check to see whether you still need to consider these projects. It could be that the answer is no. If you're not sure, move the project to the parking lot, Section 8.1, *Keep a Parking Lot of Projects*, on page 103. Whatever you do, remove projects that you don't need to consider now. At some point, you can address the projects in the parking lot. But keep projects you don't have to consider out of your immediate decision making. Don't waste your energy on decisions you don't have to make right now.

4.2 Decide to Commit, Kill, or Transform the Project

Once you've decided you should do this project, you have a limited number of decisions to make. You can commit to a project, kill a project, or transform a project to increase its chances of success.

Making a commit/kill/transform decision requires data about project progress, project value, and obstacles. If your projects are all using a serial life cycle, the data doesn't exist. In a serial life cycle, you have no data about whether this project is valuable until very near the end of the project—after you've spent virtually all the money and assigned people to this project, excluding other potential projects.

Schedule games occur often in serial life cycles. Schedule games can occur in other life cycles, but serial life cycles hide the games longer. For example, if your project teams have been implementing through the architecture instead of by feature, they run a high chance of encountering the 90% Done schedule game near the end. If you're a manager responsible for a number of serial life-cycle projects, you may have succumbed to the Split Focus or Pants on Fire schedule games as a way to manage the risk of any one project being a true failure. If you feel you have no other choices in life cycles, please read "What Lifecycle?" [Rot08b] or the appendixes in *Manage It!* [Rot07] and reconsider. And, read *Return on Software: Maximizing the Return on Your Software Investment* [Toc05] to try to do the project evaluation math that a serial life cycle requires.

A project team that chooses any life cycle other than a serial life cycle can provide you with data about the project much earlier than a serial life cycle. And, because they can provide data, they also receive feedback about the work and risks in the project and can manage those risks by reorganizing, replanning, or even redoing the work. You can manage the project portfolio with a life cycle other than serial.

Let's examine each of the decisions: commit to, kill, or transform.

4.3 Commit to a Project

When you commit to a project, it's a real commitment, not a partial commitment. Here's what a real commitment means: that until you make another conscious portfolio decision, you commit to funding this project. You commit to assigning the necessary people to the project—and only to this project. If the project needs something else (space, capital equipment, desks, whatever), you commit to delivering that to the project.

When managers don't fully commit, they revisit their projects again and again. This creates both management debt and project technical debt. They also create capacity debt because people (managers and technical) can't improve their capabilities when they're overburdened with too much work.

Recommitment Is Easy Now
by Sam, Scrum Master

We just finished our management review with senior management. Now that we're using agile, we take only about five to ten minutes to explain our status in the meeting. We just show them our velocity and a demo. I let them know about project-level obstacles. Management calls them *risks*—which is fine with me.

Our management meets with us only quarterly, because our market isn't changing that fast, so quarterly is fast enough. But it takes me only about ten minutes to prepare. The hardest part is noting what has changed in the product since the last time we demo'd. Once we demo and show our velocity data, management recommits to this project, assuming there is more valuable work on our product backlog.

Before we moved to an agile life cycle, it took us a full week to prepare for the meeting, and then our management took hours and sometimes days to decide whether we should finish a project.

4.3.1 Understand the Requirements of Commitment

A commitment to an ongoing project is not a blind commitment. If the project requires two DBAs and you have only one available because the other is on another project, think about your options.

If you have agile teams that have been fully staffed up until now, let the team tell you what they need. Sometimes, the team needs to have a conversation with the product owner about organizing this much database work into this iteration's backlog. Sometimes, the team will estimate more time for the features so that other people can learn more about what the DBA does. With those discussions, the product owner might make other decisions.

What I most often hear is not a discussion about which features to commit to when but a blind request or demand from people who say, "We need these features now." If you are not working in an agile way now, it's easy to encounter those demands. If you or your team receives a demand for this feature now and you don't have another DBA, you have to decide which project is more important than the other. If you can't fully commit to a specific project, don't start it in this time period. Wait until the next time you evaluate the portfolio.

You might tell the project team you are happy with their progress and the potential value on the product backlog, you recommit, and they continue. If you're ready to recommit to an ongoing project, do so. If you're ready to commit to a new project, do that. If you're not ready to commit, you might need to kill or transform the project.

4.3.2 Commit Fully

Commitment is not a "We'll give you part of what you need, but. . . ." It's a full commitment.

This is a hard line. Here's the problem. If you can't fully commit the necessary people and money to a project, you are guaranteeing the project will not provide the value you want it to provide. Why would you waste your people, time, and money on a project you can't fully commit to? If you have open reqs and you haven't filled them yet, know that part of the value the project team will provide to the organization is the interviewing and hiring work. You won't get the benefit of those people on the project, but the project will be providing value to the organization.

But if you don't have open reqs and if you know you need more people, you are fooling yourself if you think you can somehow commit to a partially funded or staffed project. You would be better off, from a throughput perspective, either having generalists or having at least a pair of specialists so you can fully staff a project when you need to do so.

If you are trying to staff a project with people who are working part-time on your project and part-time on other projects, you have an uncommitted project. That's because the cost of context switching will erase any potential ability to focus on this project. Don't partially commit to a project; that's a lack of commitment. Be honest. Take that project off the committed list. You may have to move the project to the parking lot. You might have to transform it. But never make a partial commitment.

4.3.3 Not Filling a Req Costs You Real Money

You have twenty projects you want to staff. You have people to staff ten of them. You also have enough open reqs to staff another five. And, you know that to interview will take time away from the people on the projects. What's a leader to do?

First, try to avoid this problem of having to hire many people. Hiring costs you time and money and slows down people on the projects. The project delays are not just from interviewing; they also occur when you bring someone on and have to train that person (see *Hiring the Best Knowledge Workers, Techies & Nerds* [Rot04a]).

If you are faced with the problem of open reqs and too many projects and a decision to hire, try this approach. First, look at your top-ranked project. Can you fully staff all of those projects? If you can, do. When you stop being able to fully staff and not disturb already-jelled teams, start hiring for the higher-ranked projects.

As you hire for those highest-ranked projects, keep the other projects in mind. If you find someone who will fit in another project, great. But watch out for hiring just for the lower-ranked projects. You might be hiring people who don't have the skills to finish more valuable projects.

> ## Two Part-Time People Do Not Make One Full-Time Equivalent
>
> If you are trying to staff a project with people who are working part-time on your project and part-time on other projects, you have an uncommitted project. Don't do that.
>
> You may have heard of the term *full-time equivalent* (FTE). Originally it was used by accounting departments to explain that several part-time staff added up to one full-time person. Gradually, it moved from part-time staff to multitasked staff.
>
> The problem is that if you have two people, each half on your project and half on another, you don't have a half-time person at all. You might have someone who's closer to 40 percent. If you're unlucky and each of those people are context switching like crazy, you might have the equivalent of 10 percent of a person. But you definitely do not have one FTE.
>
> Some number of multitasked people are not an FTE. Some number of part-time people who are assigned to just one project could be close to some number of FTEs, because they don't have the cost of context switching. But counting multitasked people is wrong arithmetic.

Remember, the projects you've ranked higher return more value to the organization. If you can't fully commit to those projects, the organization loses that value. For many of you, that's real money.

4.4 Kill a Project

Your second possible decision is the decision to kill a project. The key to killing a project is to make sure all activity associated with the project stops. Sometimes, that's harder than it should be. (See Section 4.5, *How to Kill a Project and Keep It Dead*, on page 40 for more information on good ways to kill a project and keep it dead.)

If the need for this project has changed, it's time to kill the project—and just the project. Move the people to another project. You may find that if a project is too ambitious, you'll have to kill it. Or, it may be that the market has vanished or your organization's strategy has changed.

The most serious form of killing a project is to stop all work on the project and throw away all of the intellectual property associated with

Don't Recommit Because of Sunk Cost

Sunk cost is not a good reason to commit to a project again. In fact, you might need to kill the project and not throw money away on it anymore. When you hear "But we've already spent so much on this project," that's a cue to reconsider any more commitment.

If sunk cost keeps projects alive, reconsider your ranking mechanism (see Chapter 5, *Rank the Portfolio*, on page 47). You may need a different ranking approach.

And, consider closing the project quickly if you think you must finish something to take advantage of the value created so far. An iterative-incremental life cycle for the project makes this possible.

that project—not the people, just the code or tests or drawings or whatever you have as intellectual property. Don't throw away the people. Assign them to other projects.

Postponing a project is another form of killing the project. If all the team was supposed to do was learn about an architecture or proof of concept or your customer doesn't want that project now and won't fund it, you can postpone the rest of the project, realizing there will be a startup cost later if you choose to restart it. You can choose to put this project on the parking lot (Section 8.1, *Keep a Parking Lot of Projects*, on page 103) if you don't want to lose track of it.

The kill decision is difficult to make when you're using a nonagile life cycle. (Any decision is difficult with a serial life cycle. You have more data with an iterative or incremental life cycle. You have the most data with an agile life cycle.) If the project teams don't have to get to releasable product at the end of every iteration, the project team will have some putting-away work before it's safe to kill the project. This is where many project teams and managers get confused. How much time do they need to clean up? No matter how much time you give them, it's not going to be enough, which is why I recommend you give the project team no more than two working days. At the end of two working days, ask the team to conduct a retrospective, and assign the project team to another project.

My Project Was Canceled, Parked, and Restarted
by Vu, Project Manager

We started a new project, trying for a particular kind of communication product. We had to achieve a certain level of performance and reliability. We tried a number of ideas for several timeboxes, but we encountered the "laws of physics" and just couldn't do what we needed to without different hardware. So, our project was canceled.

In another company, that might have been the end of the story. But our managers knew we had to keep this project in mind, so it went onto the "parked projects" list. I'd thought that's where projects went to die, but every quarter our managers assessed this list. One day, my boss came to me and asked about a new chip he'd heard about. Would it work on our project to give us the speed we needed? I had no idea.

At the next portfolio evaluation review meeting, our project was reinstated. We had a couple of different people—it had been two years since we'd tried to do this project. But that was OK. It was cool to see that we could kill a project for excellent reasons and then reinstate it for excellent reasons.

4.5   How to Kill a Project and Keep It Dead

Think you've killed a project? Maybe you have never worked with Marty. Marty is a well-meaning manager who didn't want to kill a particular product or its associated projects because of his strong customer relationships.

I Kept Several Dead Projects Alive Until I Realized the Cost
by Marty, Group Manager

I was responsible for several products for three years. After the third year, my management decided to phase out Product2 in favor of Product4. So, I was responsible for Product1, Product2 phase out, Product3, and Product4. I was supposed to finish the Product2 phase out in two months.

Well, we did. Except, not all of our customers wanted to move to Product4. I've known these customers for years and had personal relationships with them. I wanted to be responsive, so I kept an active branch open on Product2 and provided updates to those customers for about a year. And then, my manager, Shelley, learned about project portfolio management.

Shelley realized I'd been staffing the Product2 phase out for more than a year, not the three months she'd expected. Luckily, Shelley was nice about it and didn't fire me. I'd explained that the customers had paid for support. She agreed with me and explained how the company had prorated the support from Product2 to Product4. So, I had not only delayed Product4 releases because my staff was still working on Product2, but I had used up their support time.

I was so embarrassed. I asked if we could do something for the customers, and she said that we would have to! I kept my job, but it took me a long time to get over that mistake. I'd cost the company the opportunity to transition customers to Product4. I'd spent too much money on Product2. And, Shelley kept a pretty tight rein on me after that. But I learned my lesson.

Marty is an example of managers I've met in organizations many times. Sometimes those managers are closer to the first-level manager, who don't know or understand the organization's product strategy. They make mistakes because the strategy isn't clear. Sometimes, as Marty was, they are midlevel managers who don't understand why it's so critical to work on just the strategically important projects. If you assign a value to each project, especially as in Section 5.2, *Rank Order the Projects in the Portfolio Using Points*, on page 48, these managers might discuss the relative merits of their project, but they'll follow your direction. But sometimes you have senior managers with pet projects who are unwilling to kill these projects or leave them dead.

4.6 Killing a Senior Manager's Pet Project

If a senior manager has a pet project that you think should be killed and you think that senior manager is making this decision based on personal values or feelings, you have several options:

- Ask about the strategic importance of this project. This is a good time to meet with that manager, prepared with a list of all the projects, possibly already ranked. Now you can ask, "Is this project more important than this one?" as you walk down the list. If the senior manager says yes, you can ask, "Tell me about its importance and for how long you expect it to be more important. Can we phase releases and reevaluate its strategic importance at a particular time?" If you are lucky, you can move the project to the parking lot.

- Offer to postpone it for a while for a more strategically important project. This is one excellent use of the parked projects list.

- Say yes but mean no. This alternative can get you fired.

- Say no but mean yes. This alternative either causes multitasking or trains your managers that you will do what they want without standing up for your team.

Avoid giving your senior manager any ultimatums. Ultimatums push people into positions instead of understanding each others' principles behind the decisions. For more information on principled negotiation, see *Getting to Yes* [FUP91]. Ultimatums rarely result in anything except a career-limiting conversation for you.

4.7 Kill Doomed Projects

As you evaluate each project, you might realize you have some doomed projects in your portfolio. Here are some questions to ask if you suspect your project is doomed:

- When do we need this project to release? Do we have enough time to do something useful before that date?

- Can we make progress fast enough to meet the market window?

- Do we have people with problem-space domain expertise to staff this project?

- Do we have any insights into what real customers might want out of this project?

Let's take each one of these in turn.

4.7.1 "We don't have enough time to provide anything useful."

If you haven't started a project in time to meet its release date, you are creating a doomed project. If you can't meet a project's release date, don't start it. At least, don't start it under no-win conditions. Make sure the project environment (staffing, tools, and other resources) will support the release date. One way to do that is to start a short timebox (two weeks is good), estimate the team's velocity, and at the end of the timebox see what the team has delivered for an actual velocity.

4.7.2 "We can't proceed fast enough to meet the release date."

If you can't release this project in time to meet its due date, is it worth doing anything at all for this project? Sometimes, it is worth delivering a prototype, because you can then show the prototype to the customer and gain more schedule. But if you've been working on the project and you know you can't meet the deadline, stop the project now. You have a doomed project.

4.7.3 "We don't have people with enough knowledge to staff the project."

Sometimes, you have an appealing problem with significant technical risk. Your staff might know just enough to think about this project but not enough to deliver the project. (You've met a number of almost-PhDs with that problem. Those are the people who've done all the coursework but couldn't finish their thesis because they couldn't finish the research.)

If you haven't done all the necessary investigation, you don't really know whether the project is doable. Consider rethinking your project so you have an initial goal from a short timebox of providing information to research questions, not to release a usable product.

If the project is not feasible (an "otherworld" project), see whether you can figure out how to bring it back down to Earth to what is feasible. Otherwise, this project is doomed.

4.7.4 "We don't know what real customers or users want."

If you don't know who your customers are or you haven't talked to them in six months, you will not deliver what your customers want. This is a slow but sure way to create a doomed project.

Find out who your customers are, and keep talking to them. If the customers or users don't want to see the project team's demos, you have a doomed project. Kill that project now, and put everyone out of their misery.

You might ask these questions at the beginning of a project, before you even start it. Or, if you decide to try one iteration's worth of work, ask these questions at the end of that iteration so you can avoid recommitting to doomed projects.

Review and evaluate your portfolio periodically. If you don't see some progress from the project team, you may have a doomed project. If you and the team can't figure out a way to make the project succeed, it will become a doomed project.

4.8 Transform a Project

The third option is to change the project in some way and continue the project. However, this decision to continue is not a blind continue. You might say, "We need different information before we next evaluate the portfolio." That tells the project team they need to change what they're doing to provide that information.

Demos Made the Difference
by Angie, Business Analyst

We were making progress on our project but hadn't paid enough attention to how the demo looked for our management. We had what we called "hold-the-hand-of-the-demo" demo. We were early in the project and could demo, but from the inside out. We didn't have enough structure finished that we could demo from the user interface. We had to prove to ourselves that certain features would work before we organized around the architecture. But that made our demo hard to see.

At a portfolio evaluation meeting, we had to explain our demo as we demo'd the product. Management thought we were making things up and that the software didn't actually work. But it did. Our management explained they needed to see a more real demo.

We changed our definition of done from "demoable" to "releasable" and then showed them a demo the next time where we could start the demo from the GUI, not from another program. That helped our management see what we were doing.

Sometimes, the project is in trouble because of some of the project staff, such as the project manager or some team members. First, gather some data by talking with the project team, not just looking at the quantitative data. When you transform a project, it can be as small as clearing up misconceptions about the product backlog to changing the entire team. Transformation means to change either appearance or structure. Changing the team is certainly a transformation!

Sometimes, the team you have on the project is the wrong team for that project. Sometimes, the team can't make the velocity you require, or the project manager isn't helping the team—he or she is hurting the team, or the backlog needs to change based on new information. Whatever the cause, make the decision to change in the portfolio evaluation meeting, and make sure a project sponsor meets with the affected people to change the tasks or the staff.

If you have the wrong team because they don't have enough of some kind of skill, then decide whether you want to reassign the team to a different project or reconfigure the team or arrange for training. All have a cost—and the reassignment and reconfiguring have a much larger cost. Make a conscious decision.

If you desire a higher velocity, look at all the other decisions you can make with changing the makeup of the team. Does the team have everything they need in an environment? Are there policies that prevent the team from working as quickly as they should? Does the team need tools? Do you have unreasonable expectations about the team's potential velocity? Any number of things can depress a team's velocity.

Maybe you can add more people to the team. Adding more people to a team may not increase its velocity. Adding more people will change the team and has an initial cost while people learn to work with each other. Again, make a conscious decision.

Project teams don't work for many reasons. One common way is to have a person who doesn't work well with others—an *unjeller*, as in *Manage It!* [Rot07] and *Behind Closed Doors* [RD05]. If your team explains you have someone hurting their ability to work well together and they've tried everything, move that person off the team. Sometimes that person a technical team member. Sometimes that person is the project manager.

You may not realize if a person on the project is hurting the team. If you have an unjeller, do what you need to do to move that person off the team. But, maybe you have someone who doesn't fit the way you want to work.

Agile Is Not for Me
by Stu, Project Manager

Look, I'll be the first to admit it. I hate agile. I have to be nice to the team, the team makes all the decisions, and I don't get to build a Gantt chart. It's nuts. It's no way to run a project. Man, that Scrum training was just stupid.

So when they asked me to manage an agile project, I told them I was the wrong person. They asked me to try. I did. But why did I have to build velocity charts when I really needed a Gantt? What about design? These people didn't do design first. How could they possibly know what they had to do in the product? It was nuts.

I guess I wasn't so surprised when my manager explained I was coming off that project at the end of a portfolio evaluation meeting. Now I manage facilities projects! What a crock. I'm good at managing software projects, but my manager said my style conflicted with the team. I'll be looking for a new job.

If you make team changes, especially at the project or program manager level, don't be surprised if your staff decides to leave. Let them. If you have people who don't have enough flexibility to work toward organizational value, you don't want them.

Sometimes the product scope needs to change. In that case, make sure you understand what the project team is working toward and how you want to transform the project to manage that change. If the team is using a product backlog, you can discuss the backlog with the product owner. But if the team is not using a backlog, you might need to act to change scope.

When There's More Project Than Time
by Rich, Product Manager

We had a product requirements document (PRD) that told us what we needed to do for Release 5.3. And, we were implementing by feature. But we realized during the second month of feature building that we were not going to be able to fit everything from the PRD into 5.3 when management wanted to release it. We were able to raise this issue at the portfolio evaluation meeting.

I was amazed by the conversation about the release. Instead of management insisting that the team produce the work in the time, when the team showed they couldn't, management had a conversation about the release: was it more important to release on time or release all the features? The project manager had had that conversation earlier, so they quickly agreed that it was more important to release on time. They descoped the project early—something I had not seen management do in other companies.

4.9 Now Try This

- Have you asked the question of each project: should we do this project at all? If not, make sure you do.
- Can you make a commit/kill/transform decision for each project? If not, why not?
- Make a decision about each project, so when it's time to rank the projects, you are just trying to rank the projects you want to commit to.

Chapter 5

Rank the Portfolio

Now that you've evaluated each project the first time, it's time to refine your approach to the portfolio. You have a list of projects you would like to commit to. But you need to rank them against each other so that you staff only the most important projects.

The most important projects are the ones that provide the most business value. Business value might be a way to obtain more customers or retain the ones you have or create a new market altogether. It might be a way to release products faster or make more money on support or spend less money on support. Business value will be unique for your organization and your projects.

The fastest way is to rank each project according to its business value without any discussion. That would provide you with an ordinal ranking: 1, 2, 3, 4, 5, 6, and so on. But, how do you decide what the project's value is to the organization without discussion?

5.1 Never Rank Alone

It's difficult to decide which work is most valuable and should be done first. If you try making all the decisions yourself, you'll likely be wrong about something. Murphy's law says you'll be wrong at the worst possible time. You'll achieve the best results by collaborating across the organization to rank the portfolio with your peers so you can make decisions for the organization, not just for yourself. See *The Wisdom of Team: Creating the High-Performance Organization* [KS99] and *Wisdom of Crowds* [Sur05].

Even if you are the CEO, bring in your senior management so they understand why you rank projects the way you do. If you're not the CEO, you need to collaborate with others to make sure you can finish the projects that encompass the products your organization wants to release. If you're a first-level manager or a technical leader, you need to support your manager's mission.

One way to collaborate is to bring in a draft portfolio that you've developed yourself. This doesn't sound much like collaborating, but it is a way to help other people see what you are thinking and why you think certain projects deliver more business value than others. Don't fall in love with your draft or assume you can stop with your draft; engage others in discussing it. Then you can decide together, as in Chapter 6, *Collaborate on the Portfolio*, on page 69.

If you work in an organization where all your managers don't want to decide, you can decide. But before you decide without them, consider facilitating their decision making—if they will let you. Remind them that you don't have to all be thrilled with the current portfolio; you all have to live with it only until the next evaluation time, a form of limited consensus. The more often you iterate on the portfolio (as in Section 7.1, *Decide When to Review the Portfolio*, on page 91), the easier it will be to reach consensus about which projects are most important *for now*.

5.2 Rank Order the Projects in the Portfolio Using Points

One easy way is to use points to rank the projects. Points help you see the relative business value and ignite discussion about the relative value of each project. When you rank with points, you're separating business value from funding. The number of points you assign to a project is a representation of its value to the organization, not the funding you will provide. This separation of value from funding works in a similar way that separating project sizing from duration helps project staff estimates better.

Start with a large total number of points. You will assign a unique number of points to each project, showing its relative value to other people. The larger the total number of points, the easier it is to see each project's relative value. If you have up to eight projects, you might be able to use just 10,000 points. If you have more than eight projects, start with 100,000 points. If you have thirty or more projects, partition them in some way—by division or team or by internal or external—because it's close to impossible for human beings to understand that many projects and their relative value at one time. If you can, partition the ranking to no more than ten at a time; five to seven projects at a time is best.

Now, assign a unique point number to each project. The number of points you assign to a project helps you see each project's relative rank in relationship to all the other projects. Since I said not to rank alone, I'm assuming the "you" here is a group of you. Don't expect everyone to be in complete agreement with everyone the first (or even second or third) time you try to assign points to any specific project. Each person will benefit from the discussion of how to decide how many points a project receives. Consider adding the issues discussed later in this chapter to the point discussion; see Section 5.4, *Rank the Projects by Risk*, on page 55; Section 5.5, *Use Your Organization's Context to Rank Projects*, on page 56; Section 5.6, *Who's Waiting for Your Projects to Be Completed?*, on page 58; and Section 5.7, *Rank the Work by Your Products' Position in the Marketplace*, on page 59.

If you have two projects that are critical to the success of your organization, you might decide to assign one 5,001 points and the other 4,999 points. (Or, if you don't mind points left over, you could assign one project 5,000 points and the other 4,999 points.) That would show everyone that no one needs to work on any other projects and that these two must be completed before considering work on any others. The project with 5,000 points needs to be completed first. You would figure out how to create two teams to work on these projects simultaneously. I'm not saying to create one team to work on both projects simultaneously; that's multitasking. But I am saying that if these two projects are by far the most important work you can do for the organization, then you would staff these two projects to the exclusion of all other projects and have the two teams work on them concurrently.

With just two projects, if you have only enough staff to work on one project at a time, you can even ask the project staff to work in one-week or two-week timeboxes, alternating on each project. If one project becomes more valuable, you can decide *then* to have the staff work on just that one project for more than one timebox, assuming you review the portfolio after every timebox. See Section 7.1, *Decide When to Review the Portfolio*, on page 91 for more information on how often to review the portfolio.

What if instead you have a situation like this?

Project	Points
Project 1	3,500
Project 2	3,000
Project 3	1,000
Project 4	780
Project 5	770
Project 6	550
Total Points	**10,000**

Here you have two projects that have a relatively higher priority and a whole bunch of other projects with low point values. You have more choices now. One great choice is to fully staff the projects worth 3,500 and 3,000 points. Now you see who you have available. If those people can start work on the 1,000-point project and make sufficient progress without interrupting anyone from the top two projects, great. Staff the 1,000-point project. But if they can't make progress without needing help from the top two projects, either don't start *that* third project, because it's not that valuable, or ask those people to work on one of the top two projects. Or, ask them to work on the next project down on the list. When you have two clear winners in the ranking and a number of other much less valuable projects, do what you can to complete the first two ranked projects *without distraction.*

You might find that those "extra" people can work on the top two projects in ways you might not have considered before, such as breaking the product backlog items for each project into smaller chunks so you can have more people working in small groups on small features. Or, maybe the "extra" people can pay off some technical debt somewhere or something else that does not require an interruption for the top two projects. Don't overstaff one of your top two projects, and don't understaff any other project just to keep people busy.

Is there an ideal team size? Maybe. Schwaber in *Agile Project Management with Scrum* [Sch04] says seven people give or take two is the right number. In *The Mythical Man Month: Essays on Software Engineering* [Bro95], Brooks discusses a ten-person team. Katzenbach, in *The Wisdom of Team: Creating the High-Performance Organization* [KS99], says the number is "less than ten." Weinberg[1] says there is a factor of three with teams, and teams larger than nine break into groups by themselves. My experience with teams is that teams smaller than five people may not have enough people to finish features, and teams larger than nine break apart into subgroups.

If you add more people to a project in the hopes of finishing it faster, you may well slow it down. Every time you add more people to a project, you increase the number of communication paths. Don't move someone on to a project just to keep them busy. Optimize at the team level to ensure finished projects so you don't create bottlenecks as in *The Goal* [Gol04]. To see more about productivity, take a look at Section 10.10, *Measure Capacity by Team, Not by Individual*, on page 143.

Keeping people "fully productive" if they can't add value to the most valuable projects is not keeping them productive or adding value to the organization—it's splintering the efforts of the people who are adding value. To see more about productivity, take a look at Section 10.10, *Measure Capacity by Team, Not by Individual*, on page 143.

This is the whole point of going through the aggravation of relative ranking of all the projects in the portfolio. You know what's worth your time to start. You know what's *not* worth your time to interrupt. You know which projects you have to staff now and which ones can wait until later.

5.3 Leftover Points Provide Metadata

As you rank the projects, you might find you have points left over. That's fine. There's no rule that says you need to use all your points. Beware, however, of a lack of high-demand projects. You can think about your projects in this way:

- Projects that keep the lights on—that support the organization
- Projects that grow the business
- Projects that create new opportunities

---

1. In personal communication

Are any of them high-demand projects? If you have more projects that keep the organization running and no projects that grow the business or that create new opportunities, you may not have high-demand projects. Review your mission (Section 11.3, *Define an Actionable Mission for the Organization*, on page 149), or initiate some strategic planning to see how to grow or create new opportunities.

If you have many points remaining, say up to a third of your points, it's time to review your mission to see whether you should consider other projects. Many points remaining might indicate no one is demanding your projects. How do you provide value to the organization? Consider and propose projects that reflect that value.

Or, if all the projects have a relatively small number of points, other people in the organization don't care much about these projects. Again, review your mission to see what other projects you might offer to move the organization forward.

A project portfolio with projects that aren't valuable enough to have people clamoring for each of them is a sign that your organization is losing sight of its strategy or mission—or that the marketplace doesn't want what you offer. The more "keep the lights on" projects you have, the less people care about your projects. Reconsider where you're headed.

I bet you have many more than two projects. As you assign points, make sure each project has some point value—unless a project has no value. In that case, remove the project from your portfolio list now. That's why it's worth asking the question for every project: "Should we do this project at all?" (see Section 4.1, *Should We Do This Project at All?*, on page 33 for more information). Read Section 4.5, *How to Kill a Project and Keep It Dead*, on page 40 for ways to kill projects and keep them dead. Now, you can rank order the projects you want to consider.

Now that every project has a unique number of points, identify the highest-ranking project, and assign a team to that project. Proceed down the project list, assigning a team to each project, until you have no more teams to assign to a project.[2]

When you assign teams, assign an entire cross-functional team so that the project is fully staffed. Staffing a project with just developers or just testers doesn't provide you with a "completed" project—it means

---

2. If your organization has been agile for a while, let the teams self-assign.

Project Costs Can Affect Ranking

If you're trying to decide whether to bid a fixed-price contract or if you have a limited budget for your projects, you may have to estimate the cost or duration of a project when you are measuring its value of the project.

First, you can start a project for a short timebox, measure its velocity, and see whether you want to continue it. Second, you can talk to your customer if it's a fixed-price bid and explain that if you have to guarantee a fixed price, your price will have to be high enough to manage your risks. That's not a good deal for the customer, so maybe you can do a little, get some feedback, and refine the total price along with the date and the feature set as you proceed. If you have a team that knows about agile and has practice working in timeboxed iterations, getting to releasable product, you can show your customer your progress and explain the cost of a timebox. Then, it's the customer's decision about how many timeboxes and how many features. The third alternative is to stop using projects and rank each feature, as in Section 9.4.1, *Fix the Number of Tasks In-Process, Kanban-in-the-Small*, on page 118. Here, the customer pays by feature.

You can't definitively predict any project's cost before you've started it. You can estimate the project's cost, preferably with some experience delivering a chunk of value. (For other estimation approaches, see *Manage It! Your Guide to Modern, Pragmatic Project Management* (Rot07).) You can work with your customer to bound the project's cost as you proceed. You can work on pieces of functionality for all of your customers—one at a time—until you've finished the work the customer wants to pay for.

But don't think you can accurately predict project cost. You can't. No one can. If you think you must, make sure you add plenty of padding, because no matter what you add, it won't be enough. A better idea is to work feature by feature, reassessing and, if necessary, reestimating your project at the end of every feature.

\\/ **Joe Asks...**
⅔
  Who Should Assign a Value to Each Project?

In an ideal world, there would be a group of people with the responsibility to decide the relative value of each project. These people would meet often enough that you would always know how each project is ranked. In some organizations, a project management office (PMO) does this. In other organizations, product management does this. Some agile organizations ask their product owners to get together and rank. In other organizations, your senior managers would do this. But your world may not be ideal.

If you don't have someone else to rank order the projects, rank order them yourself, using the approaches in this chapter. Even if you're wrong, you've provided the organization information about what's not first. Use your mission (as in Chapter 11, *Define Your Mission*, on page 147) to help guide you. You can always ask for help from your peers to help you assign points.

No matter what, make sure *someone* decides on the rank ordering. Otherwise, you won't know which projects to start and finish first.

---

you have unknown technical debt because the project staff isn't getting feedback from the other people who help create an entire product.

If you're a functional manager, you can't assign a cross-functional team to each project, because you don't have responsibility or authority for those other people. In that case, make sure your ranking reflects the value of the project to the entire organization, not just your group. And, work with your peer functional managers, as in Chapter 6, *Collaborate on the Portfolio*, on page 69, so you and your peers are all staffing the same projects at the same time for the most value to the organization.

You will probably run out of teams before you run out of projects. If you have more people available than projects to finish, make sure you've staffed the projects with enough people, and revisit your mission, Section 11.3, *Define an Actionable Mission for the Organization*, on page 149. You might not be considering all the projects you could offer to the organization to add value.

5.4 Rank the Projects by Risk

If you're working with other people to decide about the project portfolio for the organization, recognize what senior management needs to know: the risk of doing this project, what the project will provide, and whether the return outweighs the risk.

You may have seen risk/return decision matrixes like this before:

Return/ Risk	High Return	Low Return
High Risk	High risk, high return	High risk, low return
Low Risk	Low risk, high return	Low risk, low return

You're not supposed to start the high-risk projects, because they're too risky. You're not supposed to start the low-return projects, because they don't provide enough value to the organization. I have two questions, and I bet you do, too. How are you supposed to know in advance? And, is there a way to start some of those high-risk projects and *see* whether they are as risky as you think they are or have the potential to return as much as you think?

You can't know in advance of starting the project. But you can start a project for a short timebox, ask the team to measure their velocity and report on their obstacles, and ask them to predict their future velocity. You can even leave those projects for several short timeboxes before you actually assess the relative risk of the project.

In all honesty, the only projects that are too risky to start are the ones that can't return anything you can see in a few weeks. Once you can see some progress (or lack thereof), the project is no longer as risky because you know how long it took for you to see this much progress. Now you just have to evaluate the potential return.

This means that the period in which you want to reevaluate the portfolio dictates how long your waterfall life-cycle projects can be. If you want to evaluate the portfolio every quarter, your waterfall projects have to be no longer than a quarter in duration. Otherwise, you're not being honest about the portfolio evaluation.

 ︶ **Joe Asks...**

 Why Should I Consider Highly Risky Projects?

Highly risky projects may offer you opportunities you may not have considered, such as helping you either consolidate or expand your business capabilities and offerings. Consolidating your business helps you refine your mission and refine your strategic planning so you can keep your projects focused on your core market. Expanding your business helps you find new markets and customers. Healthy organizations both consolidate and expand, possibly at different times. But what they don't do is *only* consolidate, reducing all risk and opportunity.

If you're not considering any risky projects, you have a limited life span as an organization. If you always play it safe, you're preventing the organization from moving forward in any dimension. After a while, you'll have only risky projects. You won't have enough data about the true project risk or value to select from among them.

If you're in a position where you have only risky projects, use agile and lean approaches to reduce the risk of starting them. Choose the project with the most risk and the highest potential return and start work in short timeboxes, making sure the project team knows you want to see demonstrable progress at the end of every iteration.

Many of the high-return projects are high risk, which is why I suggest you forget the idea of looking at risk at all. Manage the risk by using an incremental or, even better, agile approach to the project. Start with your organization's context of what moves the organization ahead instead of risk.

5.5 Use Your Organization's Context to Rank Projects

Sometimes, assigning points is too difficult, or you really can't tell which project is most valuable. In that case, look at the entire context: where you are as an organization regarding your portfolio management, who's waiting for your product to solve their problems (and reduce waste), your product's position in its life cycle, and the overall health of the product development organization.

5.5.1 Define Your Organization's Context

If you're new to managing the portfolio, you may have a bazillion projects, all of which are emergencies and all of which need to be done *now*. In that case, you will have to make choices, but you'll need to look at who's waiting for which release, how many products you have, where they are in the marketplace, and the overall health of your organization.

When you look at who's waiting for your running, tested features—your customers—you may be able to define who is more important. You can use who's more important to help you rank the projects. It's not always a C-level person, such as CEO, CFO, COO, or any senior manager, who's most important. It may not be Very Important Customer if you're in a product development organization. Sometimes, you need to do work that's blocking your ability to produce products.

> **Our Most Important Project Was the Build System**
> *by Drew*, Senior Architect
>
> We were having a terrible time releasing products. Our releases got longer and longer. We had at least thirty projects in the pipeline, and customers were screaming for more releases. We decided we had to rank the projects so we'd know which ones to do first.
>
> Because our builds took longer than three weeks to complete, we decided that spending a month fixing the build system would help us release products faster, so that became our top-ranked project. I, along with three other senior people, worked on it for one month. Between adding a few more computers and a rearchitecture of our build system and a little rearchitecture of the main product, we'd gotten the build system down to building in a day. It wasn't perfect, but that was enough to allow the product teams to make progress much faster.
>
> We actually did calculate ROI for the project. We'd originally thought we would save about thirty person-days a month. Turns out we saved about 100 person-days a month. We had no idea how much our build system had been costing us. We would have just kept complaining about it and living with it until we looked at all the work and realized we couldn't move toward a more agile approach for any of our projects until we fixed the build system.

Some organizations have many products in various stages of their lifetimes. You may have only one project team attempting to develop new products, adding new feature sets to existing products, and fixing what needs to be fixed for more mature products. In that case, you need to look at who's waiting for your projects to be completed and who's feeling the pain of the waste in the products.

5.6 Who's Waiting for Your Projects to Be Completed?

If you are working in an IT organization, you may know who your customers are by name. Some of them might have titles such as CFO or CEO. And, although it's tempting to finish projects for people in the organization who are C-level people, they may not need the projects done as much as some of the other people. If you're working in a product organization, you likely have people who represent your customers (product managers or product owners) in addition to your other managers.

Whoever your customers are, the base question is the same: "How do you calculate the value of the projects to each of your customers?" One way is to look at the waste in your customers' current work now. You can build a waste matrix that helps you quantitatively evaluate the current waste.

Project	Kind of waste	Relative importance of eliminating this waste to your company	# total customers	Value= total customers * kind of waste * relative importance to your company	Trigger date: After this date, there's no point in delivering the product	Relative value for managing this waste as opposed to all the other projects
Build System Performance	We can't build every day or even every week so the changes pile up	We can't release more often than once a year and that's optimistic. We need to release every six months	75 developers, 30 testers	105 people will be able to work in a more flexible way	We can't do release 6.5 without this	This project will helps us do all the other projects

Too often, we forget that waste begins at home. I bet you have projects on your list that will reduce your staff's waste. Those projects are the "figure out how to automate the testing" project, the "rearchitect the build system" project, and the "measure the performance for this scenario so we know why when we touch that code performance tanks" projects. Use the waste matrix to calculate your staff's wasted time to rank those projects. That matrix will help you move those projects higher up on the portfolio.

5.6.1 Qualitative Questions That Help You Determine Waste

Start with the qualitative questions, no matter whom you ask. The qualitative questions help you see the problems your customers are trying to manage.

- What kinds of workarounds are you using now?

- After this project is complete, what changes?

- Do we know what success looks like for this project?

5.6.2 Quantitative Questions That Help You Determine Waste

Once you've finished with the qualitative questions, ask questions about data.

- How will this project affect revenue?

- How will this project help us acquire new customers or retain existing customers?

- How will this project reduce our operating costs?

- How will this project move the organization forward?

Once you know the answers to these questions, your customers can calculate *their* ROI. Listen to them. If they can't see enough value to somehow increase revenue, obtain or retain their customers, or reduce their operating costs, your product has little value for them.

5.7 Rank the Work by Your Products' Position in the Marketplace

If you're selling a product outside the organization, you may have a tough time calculating your customers' waste, especially if you're trying to decide which feature has to be built when. Yes, that's part of the product backlog decision, but if some of your customers are clamoring for feature 10 and others are clamoring for feature 47, which one do you really do first?

The key is to review where your product is in its marketing life cycle.

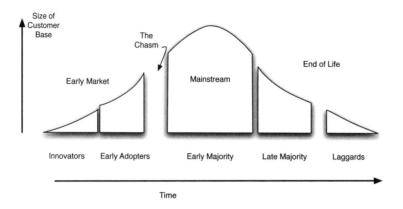

The earlier you are in Moore's marketing model *Crossing the Chasm* [Moo91], the more you have a wide variety of customers who want a lot right now. In that case, take your loudest customers (people who will be reference accounts), ask them where their waste is, and finish those projects. The more iterative and incremental the projects are, the faster you will finish their projects and be able to go on to the next projects.

Once you've hit the early majority, you don't need to release a given product as often as you do before the chasm. But it still makes sense to finish projects internally so you have choices of when to release which product for which marketplace. Now you can ask your best customers where their waste is so you can make your choices.

Those early adopters are valuable customers, but you need to be careful. The more you ask them what they want, the more they think you have promised them something. That's a problem when you reach a larger audience and the early adopters still think they have the same influence and that you've promised them features. Careful management of your project portfolio can save you here.

5.8 Use Other Comparison Methods to Rank Your Projects

If you can't use points or it's too hard to calculate waste, you still have several choices to rank your projects. Try pairwise comparison, single elimination, or double elimination.

5.8.1 Use Pairwise Comparison to Rank Projects

For pairwise comparison, make a simple list of all the projects. For our purposes, a project is a unique release of some collected set of features. (That specification may be vague where you work.) If you wrote your projects on stickies when you were collecting all the work, as in Section 3.1, *Know What Work to Collect*, on page 21, this part is easy. If you didn't make stickies or index cards before, make them now.

Place all the stickies on a wall. If you're using index cards, put them on a table. Take two stickies. Hold them up so everyone can see them, and ask, "Which one of these is first compared to each other?" Of the two projects, one is a higher priority than the other. Put the higher-priority project at the top of the list, and put the next one underneath it. Now, take the third project. Compare it to the first project: "Which one of these is first compared to each other?" If the third is higher priority than the first, put it at the top of the list. If the first one is still top priority, compare the third to the second. Keep going until you've looked at all the projects and compared them to each other. At the end, you have ranked your entire project list.

This is just like what the eye doctor does when you're being fitted for new glasses. My eye doctor says, "Which one of these is clearer: this one or that one?" first for the left eye, then for the right eye, and then finally for both. You have to make only one decision at a time. Imagine if you had to look at each image with each eye before she changed both at the same time. Too confusing.

5.8.2 Consider Single- or Double-Elimination Tournament Decision Making

Sometimes you have groups of projects and need to pit some projects against others before looking at the entire picture. This is especially helpful if you have groups of projects serving different constituencies.

A colleague in an IT group explained, "We have internal projects for our finance and sales groups, but we have external projects that allow our customers to update their information via our website. We have to organize the projects into internal projects and external projects, evaluate them inside their groups, and then compare against the groups." Single-elimination or double-elimination tournaments may help.

In single-elimination tournaments, such as in tennis tournaments, you start by pitting each project against another project. The "winner"—the higher-priority project—goes on to the next round. In the previous single-elimination picture, you can see of the eight projects, "Project 3" comes out as the winner.

Figure 5.1: SINGLE-ELIMINATION TOURNAMENT

If you have groups of projects and don't know which group to do first, single elimination is a top-down approach to choosing.[3]

However, you might need a slightly different approach to eliminating projects from consideration. In that case, try double elimination, especially if you have many options for which projects you can staff.

Double elimination is a form of pairwise comparison and helps everyone feel as if they have fairly evaluated all projects against one another, because it forces all projects to be compared to each other. In the previous picture, the initially "losing" projects run off each other on the bottom. A project isn't "out" until it loses twice. Double elimination helps you see the first project and the second project. If you have many projects in competition for the next slots down, consider using points to help you see the relative business value of each project.

---

3. Enthiosys has collaboration games for deciding about the relative ranking of projects, similar to single and double elimination.

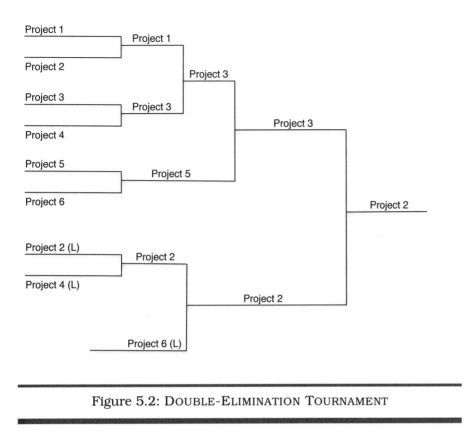

Figure 5.2: DOUBLE-ELIMINATION TOURNAMENT

5.9 Don't Use ROI to Rank

Many managers and organizations want to calculate ROI to decide how to rank or whether to fund projects. In my experience, ROI is almost always a lie or, at the least, fun with numbers. Many organizations attempt to calculate ROI as the total return for a product divided by the money invested into developing that product.

That's because for product companies who sell to a mass market—one where you cannot identify each customer—you can't predict sales over the product's lifetime. Much of the time, you can't even predict the sales for a given year. If you can't predict sales, you can't calculate your ROI, the producer's ROI. The consumer's ROI is a different question. See Section 5.6.1, *Qualitative Questions That Help You Determine Waste*, on page 59 for ways to start reviewing your consumers' ROI.

⥳ Joe Asks...

Is There One Right Ranking Approach?

No. Select a ranking approach that fits your sphere of influence and your organization's general approach to projects.

For example, if you are a group of first-level or middle-level managers and all your projects are agile, try points. Do consider your entire organization's context: the perceived relative risk of your projects, what your customers expect, who's waiting for your product, and so on. If you are a first- or middle-level manager and you're transitioning to agile or prefer an incremental approach to projects, you might need to consider more context or who's waiting for your project or who has waste you need to eliminate. If you're part of a senior management team and agile doesn't mean anything to you, single or double elimination might work best.

If the ranking approach you selected isn't working, try another approach. Remember, the more you discuss why you rank a project one way or another is most important to defining the relative ranking for each project, not the actual approach you use.

IT organizations and custom development organizations might be able to calculate ROI, but only if they have a commitment from their customers to use or buy the product and they know how many customers they will have over time. That's almost impossible for IT organizations. Custom development groups might be able to calculate ROI.

Return on investment is really a look at revenue over time. Most often, you want to understand how soon you will see any revenue and how long it lasts. That's where you need a crystal ball. You need to know how many people would buy the product, how much you can sell it for, and for how long you can keep selling the product. That's too many unknowns for me. Sure, I can make up the numbers, but even if I do, how can you believe me?

A better and simpler approach is to take a lean approach to the portfolio. Lean says, "We have finished valuable stuff. We can sell it." Once you've finished work, you can make a product to sell. Work in progress means you have nothing finished and therefore have nothing to sell.

You will still have to make decisions about which projects to fund, and for how long. The difference, once you take a lean approach, is that you have data about the current cost of the waste in the organization, or for your customers, and an approximation of how long it takes to finish a feature or a set of features. And, you might even obtain data about how long it takes to sell the product to a customer. With that data, you don't need to calculate ROI. All you need to do is look at the waste and finish the projects that reduce the most waste first.

5.10 Your Project Portfolio Is an Indicator of Your Organization's Overall Health

There are plenty of indicators of a product development organization's overall health. For the purposes of the project portfolio, you only need to look at the backlog of projects.

Healthy organizations have a number of high-demand projects. Once they have passed the startup point, they have several, if not many, projects. A healthy organization with an actionable mission has too many projects to do and has to decide among them.

If you have many projects you never finish, many projects in your parking lot you never remove, or no high-demand projects, then your organization is not healthy. Your mission may not be specific enough, or you may not know how to finish projects. You may not know what business you are in.

If you have an unhealthy organization because no one knows what to do next, consider some strategic planning. If you have too many projects to consider, review your mission, and consider some strategic planning. If your organization doesn't know how to finish projects, read *Manage It!* [Rot07].

Sometimes, the first step is to get a handle on the portfolio. Sometimes you start with a mission or with strategic planning. Start somewhere so you can finish one project and then another and another.

5.11 Publish the Portfolio Ranking

By now, you've ranked every project in your portfolio. You need to publicize that information to everyone who needs to know.

Decide whether you want to publish a ranked order of the projects along with the points like this:

Project	Points
Project 1	3,000
Project 2	2,500
Project 3	1,250
Project 4	750
Total Points	**7,500**

Instead, you could just list the rank order of the projects like this:

Project	Ranking
Data Integration	1
Performance mini release	2
Missile exploration	3
Calendar integration	4

If you have a number of projects and some of them are finishing before the next time you evaluate the portfolio, you may want to show that like this:

Month/ Project Rank	January	February	March
1	Data integration	Data integration	Data integration
2	Performance mini-release	Performance mini-release	Performance mini-release
3	Missile exploration (2 iterations)	Missile exploration (2 iterations)	Calendar integration
4	Calendar integration	Calendar integration	

I've chosen to move projects up as other projects are scheduled to complete. If that's confusing to you, don't do it.

The larger your active portfolio, the more you need to explain the relative ranking of the projects. Even if you think you have not assigned people to multiple projects, your staff will talk to each other (a good thing) and ask for help (another good thing). They need to judge where to spend their time. If a senior developer chooses to mentor a junior developer working on a higher-ranked project once a month, that might be a good use of the developer's time. If the senior developer is working on a higher-ranked project, it might not be. The key is that your technical staff understands how to best use their time and how to avoid context switching.

As you rank the projects, especially if you're building a strawman portfolio to discuss with others, define your principle behind your decisions —why you rank the projects as you do. Once you've defined your principle, you'll be able to collaborate on the portfolio.

5.12 Now Try This

- As you review each project collaboratively, make sure you ask again, "Should we do this project?" You do not need to rank a project that doesn't have enough value to the organization to commit to it.

- Can you explain to other people how each staffed project moves the organization forward?

- Try ranking each project in your portfolio with points. Are you able to rank with points? If not, what is preventing you from ranking with points?

- Test that ranking by looking at the waste you are managing and your customers are managing. Is the ranking different?

- If you can't rank in any other way, try double elimination, and see how people choose projects. Other people will choose projects based on their values, and it's helpful for you to know what those values are.

Chapter 6

Collaborate on the Portfolio

Making portfolio decisions is never a single person's problem.

To make the hard decisions about the portfolio, you need to work with other people, no matter what level you are in the organization. Since you can't make the decisions about the portfolio alone, you'll need to collaborate across the organization. When I talk about collaboration, I do mean the Webster's definition:

Collaborate: to work jointly with others or together especially in an intellectual endeavor

Collaboration to arrive at decisions can take many different forms. You might discuss, write, vote, provide data about your current thoughts, and more. For some ideas, see *The Facilitator's Guide to Participatory Decision-Making* [KLT+96] as well as *The Art of Focused Conversation* [Sta00].

6.1 Organize to Commit

Work at the highest span of influence you can in the organization, and you will maximize the return your work brings to the organization. Avoid optimizing decisions at the lowest possible level, maximizing your group's return instead of maximizing the organization's return. Instead, optimize the decisions for the organization.

> **Maximize Value for the Organization, Not Our Departments**
> *by Tony and Joyce*, Director, Software Development and Director, Software Quality
>
> As directors, we each have two primary responsibilities: to make sure our groups are producing at the highest level of capacity and to build that capacity. But we had problems with each other, because our

measurements were about our individual capacities, not building organizational capacity jointly.

Tony started, "My objectives were all about delivery date, without thinking about the quality of the product. Joyce's objectives were all about defects and the numbers of them, not whether they actually improved what the customer wanted. After a couple of years of fighting with each other, we decided to take a higher-level perspective of organizational capacity."

Joyce continued, "Once we started thinking in terms of value to the organization, we started thinking about completed work. We stopped counting things that weren't completely done and releasable. That way, Tony's features and my defects became our product."

Tony explained, "When we started thinking about whole products and working together, we were able to present a united front, convincing our management to change how we worked. We'd both been using timeboxes for our work, but when we started working together to complete first features and then projects, we were able to improve our value to the organization."

Joyce added, "Given that we have functional groups, we don't add value by ourselves. We add value when we work together to provide a complete product. We're able to work for our organization by collaborating with each other and by helping our manager see that our objectives needed to be interdependent. If our manager had insisted on measuring each of us by what only our departments could deliver as a silo, there's no way we could have provided the value for the organization. We each would have optimized what our groups could do and damn the organization. But now, we can work for the greater good, not for our personal good."

6.2 Build Trust

The biggest barrier to collaborating on the project portfolio is not how you muddle through the meeting. The biggest barrier to collaboration is lack of trust.

If your colleagues trust you, they will collaborate with you.[1] Building trust can be difficult if you've never tried to work as a leadership team before. To build trust, do these things, as suggested by *Building Trust in Business, Politics, Relationships, and Life* [SF01]:

- Deliver what you promise to deliver.
- Be consistent in your actions and reactions.

---

1. There are other barriers to collaboration, but trust is a necessary prerequisite.

- Make integrity a cornerstone of your work.
- Be willing to discuss, influence, and negotiate. Don't get stuck on your position.
- Trust in yourself and your colleagues.

To build trust with your colleagues, first identify your goal: a project portfolio for your group or organization so everyone is focused on the same work. For your team, determine how you will deliver consistently. For me, that means an agile approach to project work. Make sure you determine how your project teams will deliver.

Personal integrity, active listening skills, self-trust, and extending trust all are parts of your relationships with your colleagues at work. One way to think about all of these is to consider congruence. See Weinberg's fine description and application of congruence in *Quality Software Management, Volume 3: Congruent Action* [Wei94]. Congruence in relationships means considering yourself, the other person, and the context of the situation for each and every interaction. When you balance all three, it's easy to have integrity, to listen, and to believe in yourself and the other person. It's easy to understand but sometimes hard to do.

Here's an example of congruence. Assume you work in a matrixed organization, where the functional managers assign people to projects. If the development and test manager blame each other for the quality of the code, they are not being congruent; they are considering themselves and the context and ignoring the other person. On the other hand, if the development manager and test manager work together to determine what causes defects and work together to eliminate those problems for this project, they are congruent.

Building trust is the first step in building a collaborative team. In addition, collaborative teams show these characteristics: *Group Genius: The Creative Power of Collaboration* [Saw07]

- They have a common goal.
- They listen closely.
- They concentrate on just the issue at hand.
- They are in control of their work.
- They are willing to blend their work.
- Everyone participates.
- They are familiar with each other and the problem at hand.
- They practice their communication often.

⚡ Joe Asks...

Must I Collaborate?

You might be rolling your eyes, "Collaborate, JR? Come on. If I define a portfolio that meets my needs, why do I need to spend this time and aggravation working with other people to arrive at a portfolio that might not be as good?"

You collaborate on a portfolio for this reason: to make decisions at the organizational level—the highest level—not the lowest level. When you define a portfolio for the organization, you and your colleagues are moving the whole organization forward, not just one team or group forward.

As a side effect, you'll build relationships with your colleagues, which makes the portfolio management and day-to-day problem solving easier.

I won't be the collaboration police, checking on you. I urge you to collaborate to generate a portfolio that makes sense for your entire organization, not just your piece of it.

- They move the conversation forward.
- They learn from failure and move on.

Keep these characteristics in mind as you consider how to prepare for the portfolio evaluation meeting and how to work in the meeting.

6.3 Prepare for Collaboration

You'll be using collaboration, influence, and negotiation to arrive at a portfolio that will fit the needs of the organization.

As you prepare for this discussion, make sure you know why you ranked each project as you did—the principle behind your ranking. That information provides you with the foundation for collaboration, because you can use that principle to articulate how you think you can arrive at the team's common goal. Being able to discuss your principle behind the ranking will help you with the portfolio collaboration.

Context Defines My Principle
by Dave, Director, Software Development

I'm at a startup now, and the principle behind all my portfolio decisions is this: How do we make forward progress on the product?

Sometimes, that means we choose a few features and fix the few known defects. More often, it means how many major features and how many minor features can we put into a given release? Our portfolio management is much more at the product backlog level. When we have more than one product, I'm sure this will change.

A few years ago, when I was at a large product company, it was harder. We had several legacy products, each with tons of technical debt, and we had a bunch of long-standing customers and were acquiring new customers slowly. We had a couple of newer products where we were acquiring customers quickly. We changed our principle every quarter or so. Sometimes, we received more value by doing something to get new customers for the new products. Sometimes, it was by adding something or fixing something for our long-standing customers for the legacy products. Sometimes, it was fixing problems. But it changed based on the market and where our customers were.

Your principle can be as short as "We have to release our flagship product because it has been two years and we promised in our support contracts a yearly release." Your principle could be "We commit to projects that move our website forward for our customers so we build loyalty before we commit to internal projects."

It doesn't matter what your principle is—what's important is that you have one. Once you have a principle behind your decisions, you can collaborate, because you have a vision that's driving your decisions.

6.4 Set the Stage for Collaboration

You need this information to collaborate on the portfolio with your peers: your mission, which is what drives you (and your group) to succeed; the principle by which you will make portfolio decisions; and a strawman portfolio if you created one.

To be honest, you also need a corporate mission so you can discuss each project's value to the organization. You can't manage your portfolio without a mission because you won't have a clearly articulated big picture of where you are headed. Part of what you do might have to include defining the corporate strategy. It doesn't matter whether

> \\//
> ʒ̫ **Joe Asks...**
>   **Can We Collaborate Across Levels?**
>
> Yes, you can. It may be easier when everyone is at the same level, because no one can play the "I have more organizational power, so I win" card. But, even if someone does, as long as everyone is working toward a similar principle that optimizes for the whole organization, you will have a project portfolio that's reasonable.

you're a product company or an IT organization—you need a corporate mission to drive this collaboration.

If your organization has not defined a mission, the first part of collaboration is to define your mission. Try some of the approaches in Chapter 11, *Define Your Mission*, on page 147. Once you have a mission, you can define your strategy and refine it as you complete projects. If you have a strategy, review each project to make sure it supports the strategy, as in Section 8.2, *Conduct a Portfolio Evaluation Meeting*, on page 104.

If you've separated the projects from each other or organized them into programs, make sure you continue to evaluate the projects using one of the approaches in Chapter 5, *Rank the Portfolio*, on page 47.

6.5 Facilitate the Portfolio Evaluation Meeting

Let's assume you're in a portfolio evaluation meeting. The purpose of that meeting is to gather data so you can make the portfolio decisions across the organization. That means you need to evaluate each project, rank it, and see which projects you can commit to so you can create the unstaffed project list or the project backlog.

Everyone arrives with two pieces of data: his or her ranked portfolio and the principle by which each person ranked the projects. If you're facilitating the meeting and you are not the most senior manager, be ready for some people to be unprepared for the meeting.

The portfolio evaluation meeting has four parts: looking at each project to evaluate it, ranking each project, the commit/kill/transform decision, and the publication of the decisions. Make sure you manage each piece on its own. You may have to stop projects that are proceeding well because circumstances have changed.

6.5.1 Facilitate the Ranking Part of the Meeting

If you need some background on facilitating meetings, I recommend *The Facilitator's Guide to Participatory Decision-Making* [KLT+96]. There are three parts to the ranking part of the meeting: making sure you've collected all the work, discussing the ranking, and actually ranking the projects.

Mail an agenda like this a couple of days before the meeting so people have time to prepare.

- Part 1: Evaluate each project.

  1. Review each project's demo and velocity.

  2. Should we do this project at all?

- Part 2: Rank each project.

  1. Rank all the projects.

- Part 3: Make commit decision.

  1. Do we have enough project teams to fully commit to each project? See where we run out of people.

  2. Make a ranked list for publication.

- Part 4: Publish the ranking and expected date of the next ranking meeting.

  1. Write the ranked list.

  2. Agree on date for the next ranking meeting.

Make sure you separate all the parts. You need to see each project's state before you rank it in relationship to each other project. You need to rank each project before you can make the commit/kill/transform decision. And, you have to make that decision before you can publish the portfolio.

6.5.2 Facilitate the Commit/Kill/Transform Part of the Meeting

Once you've ranked all the projects, each manager has to make sure he or she has sufficient staff to assign to each project. This is especially challenging in organizations where managers have responsibility for functional groups, who then are matrixed into projects. If you have enough people to assign to all the projects, no problem.

But, most of the time, one or more functional managers do not have sufficient people to staff all the projects. In that case, consider asking the incomplete project team to list the lack of specific people as a risk and to transform their project.

6.6 How to Say No to More Work

As you proceed with the collaborative decisions, you may find you have too much work for the people you have available. In fact, in many healthy organizations, you do have too much work to do for the people you have available. See Section 5.10, *Your Project Portfolio Is an Indicator of Your Organization's Overall Health*, on page 65 to know whether your organization is healthy. No matter who you are, at some point you will have to say no to someone asking you to do more work. One way is not have projects at all and make all your decisions in a lean and agile way, as in Section 2.4, *Lean Approaches to the Project Portfolio*, on page 14. But, if your organization has to have projects instead of just timeboxed work, consider these approaches.

If you have a portfolio and someone—especially someone higher in authority—asks you to do more, try these approaches.

6.6.1 We Could Add More People

As you show this person the portfolio, you can say, "If we need to staff this project, we need more people." If you could add more people, either as additions to your current project or as another cross-functional team to increase velocity for the project, explain how that would work. Maybe one project should come off the current portfolio list and be moved to unstaffed work to allow the requested project to be staffed.

This is a great alternative if you have many people working solo on little bits and pieces of a project. Sometimes, a group of people swarming around a problem makes the problem easier to solve and helps the team progress faster. This is not a good idea if you are in danger of violating Brooks' law from *The Mythical Man Month: Essays on Software Engineering* [Bro95]: adding more people to a late project makes it later.

6.6.2 What Should We Drop?

It might be time to discuss the unstaffed work and see whether your ranking was successful. You can say, "Here's what we can do. What should we drop?" Once you've assigned the teams to the projects, you've staffed all the projects you can do. It's time to either reevaluate or move more projects to the unstaffed list.

This is a good time to make sure the same people are not attached to multiple projects. For managers new to portfolio management, the idea of stopping work, even just *for now*, is a foreign concept. They are tempted to ask people to multitask instead of stopping work on one or more projects. Asking what to stop doing, what to drop, is a good first step.

6.6.3 I See These Alternatives

Let's assume you've ranked the portfolio with your peers, and you all agree on what to do first, second, and third, as well as what to leave on the unstaffed list. If your manager comes to you—and only you—explain that the portfolio is a contract among you and your peers. In addition, walk your manager through the alternatives as you and your peers discussed them.

If your manager wants all of you to change your minds, explain the alternatives as you saw them and why you ranked the portfolio this way. "Here are the alternatives we discussed." Sometimes your manager can see some alternatives that you can't. Maybe you can break a current project into smaller groups of related features and have several teams work on that project in parallel. When they finish, maybe those teams can all work on this project that's not currently staffed.

6.6.4 I See These Risks

Sometimes your manager will come to you with a demand for a doomed project or a pet project. You can't make a case for this project. Try saying, "Here are the risks I can see." Explain the risks you see. This is good if you can explain risks in terms of customers.

Whatever you do, don't just blindly accept more work into your portfolio. Explain which work you will not be doing to accomplish this work.

6.6.5 Give Us One Timebox and We Can Estimate the Rest

Sometimes, a manager wants to push a project into a smaller overall duration than the project team's estimate or your experience suggests is reasonable. Instead of saying no, ask for just one timebox worth of time, where the team can measure velocity.

First, say, "If we do one timebox worth, we can estimate how long it will really take." If the team's velocity meets the project duration, you return to evaluating all the projects. But if not, this project goes on the unstaffed list.

6.6.6 Please Explain Your Principle Behind Your Ranking

If you've been working with your peers, and a senior manager (especially a CIO, VP, or equivalent) insists that you need to staff a particular project, ask that manager for his or her principle behind the selection of that project over others. When you ask for an explanation, be careful. The person hearing this can hear sarcasm or feel defensive without you meaning to sound that way. You do not want a non-career-enhancing conversation.

Showing your curiosity, say, "Please explain your ranking of this project." If the senior manager has a principle that makes sense, rerank the portfolio, and make sure everyone can live with the resulting ranking. If the senior manager appears to have a pet project, see whether the ideas in Section 4.6, *Killing a Senior Manager's Pet Project*, on page 41 will help.

Never say "maybe" to an additional portfolio request. It doesn't matter what level you are in the organization. Saying "maybe" leads to disaster. When you say "maybe," your managers hear "yes." Your peers and staff hear "no." You can't win.

6.7 Fund Projects Incrementally

Since you *commit* to a project only for a short period of time, you need to *fund* the projects only for a short period of time as well. Make sure each project has the people it needs to make progress. That's the whole point of assigning teams to projects and stopping when you run out of people (see Section 5.2, *Rank Order the Projects in the Portfolio Using Points*, on page 48). Don't starve projects of money either. Fund them money as they need it.

When my children were old enough for a clothing allowance, I asked them if they wanted all the money at once (with my heart pounding) or if I should give them money quarterly or half-yearly. They each decided

---

⋮⋮ Joe Asks...
Do You Incrementally Fund Must-Do Projects?

Sure. It's a good check-and-balance procedure. You'll know if your project team is running into trouble early. Just because you've decided you "must do" this project doesn't mean you might not change project staff to make the project run more smoothly.

---

on half-yearly. That way, they had enough money to buy fall clothes but not run out of money for the summer.

Periodic decision making about the portfolio allows you to fund projects incrementally. That's because:

- As you show value to someone, preferably your customer, you are much more likely to get more funding. This works with fixed-price contracts, internal customers, and external customers.

- If a project isn't showing value early and often, you may not get feedback early enough to change the portfolio before you start a death march for something your customers don't want.

- You can start highly risky projects because you're not committing a ton of money and time to that much risk. You're just committing two, three, or four weeks.

Because the projects show you visible progress, you have enough information to make the commit/kill/transform decision. You never have to throw good money after bad.

6.8 Never Make a Big Commitment

The big rule of project portfolio management is that you never make a big decision where you commit an entire organization to a huge project for a long time. I define huge as more than 50 percent of your people, and I define long as more than three months. That's not very big, and it's not very long. So, why am I so adamant about not making a big decision?

> ### How Can I Be Adaptive If Hardware Is Part of My Product?
>
> If your product has a hardware component, it's more difficult—but not impossible—to be an adaptive manager. You can use lean and agile approaches for projects with a hardware component also. You may have to change what done means for a given iteration while the hardware is in design. Once you have hardware in physical form, you can use adaptive approaches.
>
> If you have hardware as part of your project, start by prototyping or building what you can without hardware for as long as possible. Make sure you keep evaluating the value you're seeing as part of the project. When you need to start paying for capital expenses, or nonrecurring expenses (NREs), then—and only then—do you allocate the budget.
>
> Make sure you know something about the value you're going to receive from the project before you allocate big money. Big money means big decisions, and you want to make as few of those as you must.

In three months, if you've allocated more than half your people to one project, that project better deliver something you can see, at least as a demo. If not, you don't know whether you have three months of valuable work or three months of waste. You just don't know.

Some of you might be saying, "Look, we allocate budgets once a year. We assign people once a year. We have to plan for a year at a time." You may well do formal planning once a year, but you actually replan more often than once a year. Every time you ask people to work on another project, you are replanning. Every time you allow a support or operations problem to interrupt a project, you are replanning.

If you never have to make a big decision (a bet-the-organization decision) you are never in the position to throw good money after bad. Make your replanning explicit so you can take advantage of it, not be a victim of it.

So if you're not supposed to make a big decision, how can you make funding decisions? By funding projects incrementally. Just as you don't receive your yearly salary all at once, don't assume you have an entire year's worth of funding for your project all at once.

If you've been involved with management, you know about yearly planning and fiscal cycles. You're supposed to plan the projects—and, especially the budget—for an entire year. You're supposed to be able to predict what you need, who you need, and when you need it and when. How's that working for you? It has never worked well for me.

Instead of being a predicting manager, try being an adaptive manager. Adapting to reality means seeing data from your project teams and maybe from the accounting department if you need to track project cost. It means taking that data to predict—just for a short while—what you want to fund for projects, when you need to fund it, and how much you need. The shorter the predicting horizon, the safer the funding decisions. The longer the horizon, the riskier the funding decisions.

If you have the project teams work in relatively short timeboxes (no more than four weeks), you don't have to worry about whether a project is highly risky. The risk profile for *every* project is much lower.

6.9 Discover Barriers to Collaboration

There are times when some of your peers won't collaborate. Once you figure out why, you may be able to address the specific issues.

These are some reasons people don't collaborate:

- Someone is playing a zero-sum game.

- Someone feels as if information hiding will help their career, instead of sharing information with everyone.

- You and your colleagues do not share a common goal or strategy.

- Managers reward people for individual achievements instead of for the success of the larger group.

- You don't have enough senior managers involved who can make decisions that stick.

- People are stuck on their positions about projects in the portfolio and have not articulated their principles.

- You are not meeting in one location at one time, so the geographic and meeting distance prevents you from collaborating.

Project portfolio decisions are difficult enough when everyone collaborates. They are next to impossible if some people play zero-sum games.

To dissuade people from playing the zero-sum games, do the following:

- Make sure you have people with enough authority to make the right decisions deciding on the overall ranking of projects in the portfolio.

- Ask everyone to discuss their principles behind their ranking.

- Stop negotiating, and allow someone to "win." As long as you plan to review the portfolio on a frequent basis, reality will show the value of that decision.

6.9.1 Someone Believes in Zero-Sum Games

In a zero-sum game, someone wins, and the other person loses. People who believe that their projects must win (be ranked first) and everyone else's project must lose (be ranked last) are playing a zero-sum game.

Project portfolio management is a zero-sum game—between you and your competitors, not your organizational peers. It works when you rank the projects and collaborate at the highest level in the organization. However, if someone attempts to optimize the portfolio at a lower level, that person is playing a zero-sum game against peers in the organization.

Everybody Wins, Now
by Andrea, Director, Software Development

I've had a difficult relationship with our QA director. She didn't believe in metrics except for defects, she wanted to assign testers to the project only after all the development was "done," and she insisted that she have the responsibility for release decisions.

We started working in three-month release trains so we could release each product once a quarter. That played havoc with her assignment (and reassignment) of people to products. All of a sudden, it was clear she couldn't work the same way and allow us as an organization to release every quarter.

So, she started saying things like this in the project portfolio ranking meetings: "Well, I can assign people to that project, but if you decide what's most important, my people won't be successful. You need to let me make all the decisions."

My boss, the VP, got tired of hearing this, and finally said, "OK, you can make all the decisions for the next quarter. But here are the products I want released next quarter. You get to rank which ones go first, and we'll work with that."

Now that she had no one to fight against, she was scared that she would make the wrong decisions. She came to see me one day before the start of the quarter and asked me to review her ranking. I explained that development has less work on the projects she'd ranked 1 and 2 and that I thought the projects she'd ranked 5 and 6 would provide more value to the organization. I explained I would go along with whatever she decided. No way was I going to fight with her!

It took only one quarter of portfolio planning for her to realize we were not trying to make her lose or win—that we wanted to win as an organization, not individually. She stopped playing the zero-sum game.

6.9.2 Someone Believes in Information Hiding

Portfolio management can succeed when project teams are transparent with their progress and with what they have left on their backlog. If teams, including product owners, attempt to hide their velocity or demos or their backlog, the people who need to collaborate don't have enough information to make good decisions.

We Need All the Information to Make Good Portfolio Decisions
by Vince, PMO Director

We've been trying to manage the project portfolio for years. We'd run into trouble with project teams not telling us the whole story—mostly because they didn't know but partly because the project managers didn't provide us with all the information.

We had a project manager who refused to give us status, except for "The project is on track." I finally asked, "How do you know?" The project manager answered, "I have faith in my team."

Since we'd been working in more of a serial life cycle, that was just about all the answer the project manager could give. So, we instituted a few things: a quarterly review of each project and a demand that each project show us progress in the form of a demo. In addition, we asked to see what was left to do.

Those few requests first had the project managers up in arms, especially those who were planning to leave all the integration and testing until the end. We explained we didn't care how they organized the project, as long as they could show us a demo so we could see what was complete and what they had remaining to do.

A number of the project teams struggled, but once they decided to show us their progress and what they had remaining, the project managers reported an interesting side effect: the teams seemed to be finishing work faster.

Now, because the teams show us completed work, they are willing to move onto other projects when we say, "OK, that's enough for that project. Please release it." We have very few projects that take as long as we anticipate they will. Yeah, it took us about a year to get here. But everyone can see what everyone else has done and what's left. The project teams can see as well as we can when a project is done enough and when it's time to move on.

6.9.3 There Is No Common Goal

If you don't have a corporate strategy, you can't be successful at managing the portfolio.

Part of what you do might have to include defining the corporate strategy. It doesn't matter if you're a product company or an IT organization —you need a corporate strategy to drive the portfolio collaboration.

Once We Had a Mission, We Had a Portfolio
by Audrey, PMO Director

We had a devil of a time ranking the projects. We're an IT department in a large engineering company. We have projects for our infrastructure and projects that affect our customers. We had trouble deciding which projects to do first and which ones to postpone for a while. Part of the problem is that we didn't define the value that we as a department provided to the company.

We built our mission from the bottom up, looking at both kinds of projects, so we could talk about the value each of the groups provided to the organization. Then we discussed the departmental value we brought to the organization. What a surprise—it was a double-pronged value.

Our mission is "Create and maintain the infrastructure for the entire organization." It's not an inspiring mission, but it tells us what to work on. Now, when we work on our portfolio, our CIO first has conversations with his peers and learns about the quarter's and year's initiatives. That allows us to make the month-by-month decisions.

6.9.4 Incentives Push People Toward Zero-Sum Behavior

Sometimes your organization inadvertently encourages behavior they *don't* want. For example, some incentives encourage managers to think about their project or customer first while you really want everyone to think about the overall picture. These incentives are based on an individual's ability to push through his or her initiatives using a common pool of developers, testers, and business analysts, regardless of whether that individual's project is a higher rank than any others.

This confusion happens when an organization misapplies Management by Objective (MBO) and senior managers respond by optimizing from the bottom of the organization instead of from the top.

Competing Product Managers, Nothing Gets Done
by Max, Ruth, Development Manager, Test Manager

We're part of a centralized development group for a product group. All the developers report to me (Max), and all the testers report to Ruth. Jointly, we create cross-functional teams for the projects and work on projects. We have a standard product and several custom variations.

Several years ago, we had a deadly situation. We had three teams of people working on projects but seven product managers trying to direct our work. When we tried to talk to them about ranking their requirements so we could work on just one project per team, each one of them stonewalled us. I finally took one of them, Peter, for coffee, off-site.

"Peter, what's going on? Ruth and I want to organize the work so we're doing only one project at a time." I'd heard of people looking like they were going to faint, but I'd never seen it before. Peter paled and looked as if he was going to have a heart attack. "Max, you can't do that. My pay depends on getting this project out the door."

"Peter, we can't do what you need fast enough."

"That's not the point. I don't get paid if you're fast enough; I get paid as long as you make progress. If you stop working on my project, my pay and my bonus are in jeopardy. You've got to keep working on my project."

It was clear that Ruth and I were working at the wrong level in the organization. Ruth tried next, to work with the VP of marketing and sales, to whom the product managers reported. She had a similar conversation, with the same results. It was clear we needed to work on senior management. But not by ourselves.

We enlisted the help of our VP to bring the problem to the senior management meeting. It took us more than a year to change the MBOs for the VPs, who then had to change the MBOs for the product managers. We also got senior management to discuss why we had so many product managers and so few development teams. This transition was not easy, but once we changed the MBOs, we were able to make progress on the projects, because we had to work on only one project at a time.

The product managers now meet together as a group. They think about what they can accomplish together to meet their group performance. Now, they drive the strategy with *their* goal of using the project portfolio to optimize their product performance to reflect the organization's strategy.

6.9.5 The People Making Portfolio Decisions Don't Have Enough Authority

Even if you work with your peers, you may not have enough authority to make the portfolio decisions. If that's the case, make sure you know who is making the final decisions, and suggest a strawman portfolio you and your peers have developed.

> **We Can Suggest, Not Commit**
> *by Susan, Drew, Vinny, Sam*, Test Manager, Development Manager, Tech Pubs Manager, Project Manager
>
> We were having trouble with our projects—every single one was late, every one had too many defects, and the customers always wanted something different once they received the product. We had too many concurrent projects. So, we decided to organize the portfolio.
>
> It took us the better part of a day, but we finally came up with a ranked list of five projects. We assigned people to those projects and put the other projects on our unstaffed work list. That worked for all of three days. Then our director, Dave, came up to Susan and asked why she wasn't working on Project6. She replied at the time, "Because it's not on our list of projects to do now; it's on our list to start after these five projects."
>
> Sam interjected, "By the time Dave got to me, I thought he was going to have a stroke because he was so upset. I asked him, if he had to choose five projects, which projects would he choose, in what order?" He explained. I told him I would call the managers together and staff those projects in that order.
>
> We learned a huge lesson. We don't know everything we need to know about the portfolio. We can suggest a ranking to our management, but we can't commit to projects ourselves. It helps Dave when we give him a strawman portfolio, given what we know about the projects. But Dave and the VP get to decide, not us.

6.9.6 People Are Arguing Based on Position, Not Principle

Sometimes, when everyone brings a strawman portfolio, someone is attached to a particular project or attached to a particular ranking. If that occurs, it can feel similar to the zero-sum game. In this case, read *Getting to Yes* [FUP91]. Their negotiation scheme is to do the following:

1. Separate the people from the problem.
2. Focus on interests, not positions.
3. Generate a variety of possibilities.
4. Use an objective standard to judge the results.

This is why everyone needs a principle they can articulate before arriving at the portfolio meeting. If you and I can state our principles, we can separate the people from the problem. If you and I have different principles and we discuss that at the beginning of the meeting, we have a good chance of resolving that problem before we start fighting about the portfolio.

6.9.7 You Are Geographically Separated

If you are geographically separated and need to agree on which projects you tackle first, make sure you separate all the geographically distributed problems from each other. Let's assume you have teams who can complete pieces of functionality in their own sites and your problem is to know which features or projects have to be completed first.

If you've built enough trust as a management team or a group of peers, have one in-person meeting first to define your first portfolio. Now, you've likely built enough trust with your peers to have remote meetings for the rest of the year. However, consider using email for prework, such as each of you articulating your principle behind your choices for the portfolio, showing each other your strawman portfolios, and discussing any constraints.

For the portfolio meeting, use as many online collaboration tools as possible so you can all see the data. For example, you won't be able to see cards or stickies on the wall when some people are remote. This is knotty and delicate work. Expect your portfolio evaluation meetings to take much longer than if you could have the meeting with all of you in one place.

Unfortunately, when you have teams that cannot complete pieces of functionality at their sites and instead the team members need to rely on each other, make sure the most senior level of management decides on the portfolio. Lower-level managers and project managers have enough aggravation trying to get an entire piece of functionality done to worry about the portfolio. If you are part of that most senior level of management, I urge you to reorganize your team bits into site-based teams that can complete pieces of functionality. Until you do, you need to make the decisions about which projects are which rank, and you will need help knowing who to assign to which projects. A kanban approach, where you limit the work in progress, may help you, as in Section 9.4, *Stabilize the Number of Work Items in Progress*, on page 117.

> **Results and Relationships**
>
> As you manage the portfolio over time, you'll notice that you deliver better results to the organization and that your relationships with your managers and peers across the organization improve.
>
> The improved results make sense, but the relationships, too? That might come as a surprise to you. But your relationships improve (or make problems obvious) because you have fewer emergency projects, because you collaborate more often, and because you know how your managers and peers are judging the organization's success.
>
> That is a level of transparency you do not normally see in organizations.

This might seem like a lot of work to you. It is. You might even think you can delegate this to other managers below you in the hierarchy. Forget about it. You created a situation in which the project teams have limited bandwidth, so you need to solve this problem.

You may find you have other barriers to collaboration. Recognize that the barrier is a symptom of an organizational problem, and think about how you need to solve it.

6.10   Who Needs to Collaborate on the Portfolio?

I've been deliberately vague about who collaborates on the portfolio. In some organizations, the people who define the portfolio are the operating committee; a project management office (PMO); the senior managers, including the CEO; and rarely, the functional managers of the technical staff. Any of these groups of people can succeed. Any of them can fail.

Every time I've seen the project portfolio work succeed, it's because the group of people optimized at the highest level of the organization and worked to determine how to support the mission and goals of the organization. If you and your peers can do that, you are ready to manage the project portfolio. If you can't, determine the people who can do that, and invite them to collaborate with you. The results will be worth it.

6.11 Now Try This

- Review all the projects in your portfolio. Based on how you are organized (functional, matrix, project), how will you need to collaborate? Decide whether you need to collaborate just with your manager, with your peers and a manager (or two), or with the rest of a senior management team.

- Review how your projects are interrelated. If they are, should they be programs of some sort? If so, which kind of program?

- If you have rethought how your projects fit together in programs, make sure you reevaluate the ranking of each project and program.

Chapter 7

Iterate on the Portfolio

If you want to consciously make portfolio decisions rather than have the projects whip you around, you'll need to plan how often you will want to review and adjust the project portfolio. If you don't plan to iterate, you will have emergency projects (Figure 2.2, on page 11), which throw the whole organization and the portfolio into disarray. If you plan your iteration period, you will prevent emergencies and help the project teams make the most of their time for their projects.

When most people slot their projects into a portfolio, they easily have twelve to eighteen months of planned work in the portfolio. That's way too long. You can't possibly predict the future a year in advance.

At some point—way before you finish the projects—something happens, and you'll need to readjust the portfolio. You and your colleagues need to determine how often you need to review the portfolio so you can adjust the relative priority of each project and the staffing or funding for each project.

Reviewing the portfolio includes the actions of planning and replanning the portfolio. Your job is to make decisions as you review.

7.1 Decide When to Review the Portfolio

You can plan for the adjustment in a portfolio review, but how often should you review the portfolio? Too often, and you aggravate everyone involved, because nothing has changed. Not often enough, and the projects underway have no relationship to the list of staffed and unstaffed work. Match the frequency of your portfolio review to your development style, and make sure that if you're using a serial life cycle, you don't wait until the end of any project.

If you're using iteration boundaries for your projects, that's a good time to review the portfolio. If you're using a serial life cycle, review the portfolio at least quarterly to ensure the projects are still valuable. If you opt for more frequent reviews and decrease the project scope, you can avoid or better respond to emergencies. With an iterative or incremental life cycle, you can review the portfolio after the teams complete a prototype or a feature chunk.

If you plan to review and readjust the portfolio periodically, your project teams will adjust to your time period. That's because you need a demo and data to make decisions about committing to the project again. If you explain to the teams what results you want (a demo and project progress data) and you tell them when you need it, you will get it.

You might need to review the portfolio when release dates change, when your customers want something new, when your competitors announce or release new products, or when new technology is possible. Because you can't control most of these events, you'll need to be flexible about your review cycle. But you do have ways to decide when is the right time to review the portfolio.

The ideal time to review the portfolio is:

- When a project finishes something you can see (the project cycles)

- When you have enough information about the next version of a product (the planning cycles)

- When it's time to allocate budget and people to a new project (the business cycles)

These cycles are interdependent. Here's a true story about how one group recognized the interdependencies.

Competing Product Managers
by Leah, Product Manager

Leah, a product manager at a large company, was talking with Alex, another product manager. "Alex, I need the development team to work on my product upgrade. When are they going to be done with your product?"

"Not for another three months."

Leah sat up. "Wait a minute. You've had that team for six months already. My product needs another release sooner than that. I have requests from our customers, and the corporate road map says I need to release in just three months. If they can't work on my project, how can I get a release out in three months? What's the delay from?"

Alex sighed and said, "Well, we had trouble getting the requirements done, so that was a delay. Then we had trouble with the functional specs. It turns out the requirements were still a bit vague, so we had to revisit everything during the spec stage. I insisted that they work on all the features at the same time, so the testers can't start because nothing is done enough for them to test."

Leah stalked away from Alex and strode into her manager's office. "I need help. I won't get the project team for months. I'm so frustrated. We need to work toward the whole organization's goal, not just one product manager's goal."

Alex and his managers made several classic mistakes:

- Thinking that his project was alone—not considering the rest of the portfolio in his planning

- Insisting on a serial life cycle when there was a known time constraint for his project

- Not encouraging the project team to implement and test by feature, so they could stop at some time, even if that time was not when the project would complete all the requirements

If Leah and Alex—or their management—had reviewed the portfolio more often, Alex would have avoided the first mistake of thinking he had the only project and would have had a chance to revisit the other mistakes earlier in the project. Without *someone* making portfolio decisions, Alex quite correctly thinks he has access to all the people he needs for as long as he needs. That's fine for Alex's project, but not for the rest of the organization.

7.2 Select an Iteration Length for Your Review Cycles

Your project portfolio review cycles depend on the choice of life cycles for your projects and how long the projects are, on how frequently you need to plan or replan the product road map, and on how much budget planning and replanning you need to do.

7.2.1 Project Life Cycles Affect Project Portfolio Management

Because your review cycles depend on your projects' durations, you'll need to adjust your iteration length to match your projects' durations. If you use an iterative, incremental, or agile life cycle, you have opportunities during a given project to review and replan the portfolio. But if you use a serial life cycle, such as a waterfall or phase-gate, your portfolio review cycle is the entire duration of the project. If you contain the requirements, the team is familiar with the product, they don't run into technical difficulties, and the schedule is short enough, then you may be able to make serial life-cycle projects work for your portfolio management.

But too often, I see time-bound projects with high technical risk try to fit everything into a serial life cycle for a project that's more than three months long. That's not a recipe for success, for the project, or for managing the portfolio. Instead, consider another life cycle for your projects.

If one project takes longer than six months to complete, you are deciding not to staff other projects that might need to start, and even finish, before the team is done with their original project. If you feel enough pressure, you'll ask people to work on more than one project, leading to multitasking and waste. Help the project team choose a life cycle that fits your business requirements of when the project needs to finish and that fits your time need to review the portfolio. As an organizational leader, this is where to put your energy.

If you use an iterative life cycle and integrate the product as you proceed, leaving only final testing for the end, your project portfolio review cycle can be as short as the time it takes to implement one feature, integrate it, and test it. If you use an incremental life cycle, such as staged delivery, your review cycle can be as short as the time it takes to finish one feature. If you're using an agile life cycle, your review cycle is the duration of one timebox, not more than four weeks long.

If one of the projects in your portfolio requires many features and a tight schedule, the more you want that project team to use an agile or incremental life cycle. Because the project team completes features inside a timebox, you have the most flexibility in replanning the project portfolio. You might not care what kind of a life cycle you use for a relatively mature product, assuming you don't want to release it more often than once a year or so, and you don't need that project team for other work.

The more projects compete for fewer project teams, the more you need an agile life cycle for your projects. If you have only a few projects waiting for project teams, you might be able to use an incremental life cycle. But if you have many more projects than you can staff, it's time to move to agile. You can't get the throughput out of your teams and the ability to decide and change quickly in any other life cycle.

Two Teams, More Than Twenty Projects
by Paul, CEO

We're a small software company doing custom development, and we want to retain our independence. We can pay people the way we want and not have to answer to anyone if we stay independent. But a couple of years ago, we were in trouble and were considering looking for financing.

We had way too many projects to do and not enough time or people to do them. We had only two project teams and about twenty-two projects. At first, I told my VP that we needed everyone to work on more than one project at a time. That didn't work. So, I told him to find another way.

First, he had all the project teams work in timeboxes so we could see what they could do in three weeks. Then he changed things so they were implementing and testing by feature inside the timeboxes. That worked really well, because we could demo to the customers. If the customers wanted some time to think about it, we could say, "Take three weeks. We'll be ready for you then." We got great feedback from them.

Long story short, we started using two-week timeboxes. We still have a ton of projects—way more than twenty now—and we're able to juggle things because we know how to slot the work into the portfolio, and we can allow our customers enough time to review our work to date. Some of our customers know they have a three-month wait before we'll show them the first demo, and they are willing to wait because of how we work with them.

Now, when we close a contract, we work with our customers to slot them into the portfolio. We always have people working on only one project. And, because people are so focused on one project at a time, they really learn the guts of the product. They're much faster on that project, and they can take their knowledge and apply it to the other projects more easily.

7.2.2 Product Road Map Planning Affects Project Portfolio Management

It makes sense to make your planning cycle—the readjustment of the product road map, which features you want in which quarter—occur every quarter, especially for less mature products or for a market in flux. If you're using an agile life cycle, you can readjust the road map every timebox, fine-tuning which features the project team will finish when, as well as when you can release the product.

With an incremental life cycle, you have almost the same flexibility as with an agile life cycle, but you'll have the project startup time, plus the varying time to complete a feature. For an iterative life cycle, you'll have to allow for the time to add in all the prototypes for a given feature and test it. For a serial life cycle, you'll have to restrict the number of requirements you can address in one project to meet your need to review the portfolio.

Knowing What We Want in the Product When
by Steve, Product Manager

I've always kept a road map for my products, but I wasn't very specific about when we wanted which features. It's a big product, and I honestly thought it didn't make much of a difference, until last year.

Last year, my management finally decided to stop multitasking. They told all of us product managers that we needed to provide two things: a quarterly list of features for our products for them and a ranked product backlog for the project team. Anyone who didn't have those two pieces of information would not have funded projects for the quarter.

One guy decided he wasn't going to—he was working on the product requirements document (PRD) for the company's flagship product. They didn't fund that project for that quarter. That turned out not to be that big a deal; they'd just released a major version, and there's no way he could have finished the PRD in time for the project team to work on the project.

That made the rest of us realize our management was serious. We now all have quarterly product road maps for at least two quarters out. I have ranked product backlogs for all of my products—only the first twenty to thirty requirements are ranked, because the teams never do more than that in a timebox, and usually less. I actually have more time to talk to my customers and see what they think of our demos and what they want for the future.

As a manager in the organization, work with your peers to create or use product road maps so you can anticipate what projects need which life cycles and which people when. Use your political power to influence the project managers and first-level managers to use timeboxes wherever possible and to implement by feature. That way, as the project teams implement the features and as the product road maps evolve, you and your peers can make better and faster portfolio decisions.

7.2.3 Budgeting Affects Project Portfolio Management

Many organizations budget once a year. Everyone is supposed to pull out their magic wands and crystal balls and see the future perfectly.

Well, I don't understand how to predict the future, and I can't tell what the competitors are going to do—and neither do my clients. The result is that managers and project managers spend crazy amounts of time forecasting the budget, and by the third month into the fiscal year, the budgets are all wrong.

Since the budget is wrong in three months or less, we'll move to rolling-wave budgeting along with rolling-wave portfolio management. We'll still create a budget target for the year, but we'll allocate funds only for a maximum of three months. If you're using an agile life cycle with a shorter timebox than three months, you can have a budget cycle as short as the timebox.

Instead of thinking about the budget driving the amount of time and the number of features, use a fixed time and a fixed budget to see how much value you can deliver in that time period. The money folks commit to some money for some amount of time—as little as a month if they want—and you commit to some set of running, tested features at the end of that time.

The money people cannot change funds during this time. If you're using a nonagile life cycle and you don't have an interim deliverable for six months, the money people have to keep their commitment for six months. What happens if the economy crashes and you need to revisit your strategy and your decisions? Revisit. But, this is why an agile life cycle provides you with the most flexibility.

Most of the time, you don't have dramatic strategy changes. Most of the time, you want to make smaller course corrections that allow you more flexibility. When the money is fixed and the time period is fixed, the iteration is stable enough for the project team to create a valuable product.

A side benefit of rebudgeting more often is that you don't have to create a detailed budget for everything—you just have to budget for the foreseeable future. You'll spend less time budgeting and more time seeing just what you need.

An additional benefit is that for a nonagile life cycle, the project team has to reestimate how much longer they will need to finish the project.

Too often, project teams have no idea how much time they need. If their estimates are off, they will gain feedback on their estimates and become better estimators.

For you project managers, even if you can't use an agile life cycle, you can use historical information to organize your project and its budget. If you know from past experience that your budget will change sometime between the six-week mark and the four-month mark, you can plan to deliver something valuable, such as a demo, a prototype, or running, tested features every six weeks. That way, you've shown value each budgeting cycle. You'll get more funding. (Tricky, eh?)

We're Actually Staying Within Our Budget
by Lakshmi, IT Accounting Manager

We're an IT group, so we're on a strict budget. We used to budget once a year—what a nightmare. We tried every year to allocate money toward training or conferences, and that money got taken by projects. It was awful.

But now, we don't buy anything in advance for a project unless we're going to need it in the next month. Sure, for servers and big equipment, I need to anticipate and order early, so we actually receive the equipment when we need it, but most things we order only when we need them. So when we have new people starting, I don't buy all the furniture at the beginning of the year. That money doesn't vanish because the projects ate the money. I buy laptops and phones only when we need them. And, best of all, we have almost no overtime, so my budget predictions are darn close to accurate.

I have a predicted budget for the year—our accounting department wants to see that. But I *manage* the budget week by week, a quarter at a time, and I don't allocate money to projects unless they actually start. The CIO wants to move to monthly budgeting with a monthly portfolio review, and that will be a piece of cake for me. I bet we stick to the budget better, too.

As a senior manager, you can stop the budgeting madness. You can use your span of influence to create a rolling-wave budget and portfolio. You can help your managers drive the discipline of managing the portfolio into the project teams.

As you consider what the iteration length for your portfolio review, consider your project life cycles, how much change you have in your product planning, and how fixed your budget is. The more risk you have in budget and product planning, the more you want the projects to work in short timeboxes. That way, you can review the portfolio at the end of every timebox.

Review the portfolio as often as you can and no more often. Consider working with other leaders around the organization both to know what to do and to organize your projects so you could release something at least once a quarter. You don't have to actually release, but if your project is in a releasable state, you have the option of moving a project team to another project and satisfying the needs of the project portfolio. Then you'll be able to review the portfolio and know you can make new choices about the work the organization is doing.

7.3 Defend the Portfolio from Attack

In any organization, there are people who think they can request "extra" work from developers, testers, writers, whomever. "Can you please do this as a favor to me?" is one of their favorite lines. Too often, the technical staff say yes, because they think they're doing something good for the organization.

The problem is that people who circumvent a product backlog also circumvent the project portfolio planning. You need to defend the portfolio from their attacks.

You will have your own way of dealing with these folks, but here's what has worked for me. I requested all the technical staff work on the portfolio in rank order. If they received other requests, or requests for work not in the backlog, I asked them to use this phrasing: "That sounds great. Please talk to JR about slotting that request in." That's all they had to say. They were the good guys and could continue their work. I would work with the managers and product managers across the organization to determine what to do.

7.4 How to Decide If You Can't Change Life Cycles, Road Maps, or Budgets

You might be working in an organization desperate to start project portfolio management. Not because they know about managing the portfolio, but because they can't get anything done. You might be a first-level manager of some variety who wants to stop the multitasking madness.

If so, consider selecting a specific replanning period, such as every quarter. Quarterly portfolio management isn't the One Ideal Time, but for people starting with a lean or agile approach, it might help projects deliver value earlier.

The problem with setting a quarterly planning and budgeting cycle is that you need your projects to deliver some finished set of features by the time you get to the review. Many organizations spend more than three months getting started on a project, which is quite common in waterfall or iterative life cycles. If you're careful with an incremental life cycle, you can make a quarterly planning and budget cycle work. Only agile life cycles, with their short timeboxes and emphasis on finishing pieces inside the timebox, can work with quarterly planning and budget cycles reliably.

We're the Only Ones Managing Our Portfolio
by Ted, Director, Software Development

I have total development responsibility for several related products in our product line. I have to beg for testers and writers. We have cross-functional teams because I make the test managers and tech pubs managers assign people for the duration of a project.

I started managing our portfolio when I just couldn't take it anymore. I didn't know what everyone was working on, we weren't making progress, and I was spending too much time in meetings explaining why we were always late. I decided two things: that we would work in timeboxes and that we would work on only one project at a time.

I started with two-week timeboxes so we could finish something, even if it was just a little bit. I assigned people to just one project at a time. It took me a few weeks to get the hang of evaluating each project with my managers, but once we did, it just took us about an hour every two weeks to review and replan the portfolio. I started publishing what we would work on for the next two timeboxes, sort of rolling-wave portfolio planning.

I explained to the director of testing and to the director of tech pubs that this was how I was having my teams work. I wanted them to also assign their people for the duration of a timebox. I wasn't going to make them; I requested that they do so. I told our product manager that he had to rank requirements. I worked with accounting about the budget, but they refused to think about anything other than a yearly budgeting cycle. Fine.

It wasn't easy, but we're at a place where we have a ranked product backlog for each of our products. We still don't have road maps, so I get surprised by product changes that require budget changes, but I have many fewer of them. I have convinced the test and tech pubs folks that working in timeboxes, with a result of running, tested features, helps them, so they're along for the ride—most of the time. Sometimes, they still have emergencies, because they still haven't organized their portfolios, but they have fewer emergencies.

This would be easier if we had an R&D-wide portfolio, but we don't. But I'm managing what my folks do, and we have many fewer disasters, less confusion, and very few emergencies. Even better, we actually finish projects.

7.5 Make Decisions as Late as Possible

Maybe you've decided you'll try this portfolio management business. But you need to fund some projects now to see what they can deliver.

One of the lean principles is to defer commitment to a project until the last responsible moment.[1] The problem is, with software projects and with software/hardware combination projects, you might need to fund prototypes or some early development until you know what the project will be able to deliver.

That's OK—both to wait until the last possible moment and to fund some of the project and then decide what to do, as long as you decide what to do and know how you'll decide to keep going or stop. That decision making will differ based on where you are in the organization and how strategically you need to think or act.

One way to make decisions as late as responsibly possible is to use short, timeboxed iterations for your projects. If you use two-week time-boxes, you can see some initial progress on a clear set of work. You can reevaluate your decision about this project in just two weeks. I've used timeboxes up to four weeks long, and if we're experimenting, I find shorter timeboxes work better for my decision making and the team's progress. The short timeboxes help the team feel that I really do want to measure what they can accomplish in a short time. If they can't accomplish what they thought they could, I have some easy choices: give them another timebox or two, or stop the project right now. Two weeks is long enough to learn something and not so long that we (the entire organization) has spent time we can't afford.

---

1. I first heard this as "Make decisions at the last responsible moment" from Hal Macomber in 2003 in *Designing Breakdown-Tolerant Project Environments* at http://www.reformingprojectmanagement.com/2003/09/19/238/.

If you're really crunched for time, consider one-week timeboxes and limit the number of timeboxes to three or fewer. If you don't know enough in three weeks, you can take a bigger-picture view and assess the overall risk of this project. The waste matrix in Section 5.6, *Who's Waiting for Your Projects to Be Completed?*, on page 58 may help you see how to look at the risks of doing or not doing this project.

We Wait Longer to Start Now
by Don, VP Engineering

We are developing a new product in what I call a client-regulated industry. Our clients demand that we use third-party components that they have contracted for with other suppliers. These other suppliers provide us with components we're just supposed to be able to use. Of course, it doesn't work that way. More often than not, these suppliers don't meet their schedules. If they do meet the schedules, they don't have the features we need when we need them.

We used to staff projects anyway and wait for our suppliers to finish what they were supposed to do. But then we got the idea of waiting until the last responsible moment. Now we have two choices. We can wait to start a project until we receive the first code deliverable from our supplier. Sometimes that works. More often, we have to start a project and prototype so our customers and suppliers can see what we do. Or, we start a project and iteratively deliver the features we can do alone into the code base. Then we can postpone more work on that project, until it's responsible to fully staff it.

I would prefer to just staff the project and finish it, but that's not going to happen in this industry. At least this way I don't have to commit project money and people for an entire year. And, I start and stop projects when the team is at a good starting and stopping point.

7.6 Now Try This

- Without considering the life cycles your projects are using, how often would you like to review the portfolio? Is there any way for your projects to provide you with information that often? If not, what would you have to do to get that information?

- If your projects are not using agile or incremental approaches now, what would you have to do to make that happen?

- What would prevent you from using a rolling-wave approach to managing the portfolio?

Chapter 8

Make Portfolio Decisions

By now, you've evaluated each project and ranked it. Let's step back and reconsider the finer points of what it means to commit to, kill, or transform a project.

Making those decisions is not easy. You'll need to gather data about the projects and decide how to make your decisions. One way is to conduct a portfolio evaluation meeting. You may have heard of these as management reviews. Don't worry—this isn't the kind of management review you're used to. There won't be a dog-and-pony show with Gantt charts or traffic-light status reports. This management review is crisp and is designed to provide you with the information you need.

8.1 Keep a Parking Lot of Projects

It's probable that you have more projects than you have people to staff them. You don't want to lose track of the projects, and you may not want to keep them on the unstaffed list for your portfolio. And, if you're not going to staff them for a while, you want to take them out of consideration during the project portfolio meeting but not forget about them. That's what a project portfolio parking lot does for you—it gives you a place to put the projects without losing them or cluttering your project portfolio.

This is a good approach for people who love to cross work off their lists. They ask whether the project should be done at all, as in Section 4.1, *Should We Do This Project at All?*, on page 33, or realize they're wasting energy considering this project over and over and over again. They take the project off the unstaffed work list and off the potential portfolio. They stop thinking about it. They are done thinking about this project *for now.* This is the same thinking as in the popular *Getting Things Done* [All02].

Some people may be concerned about removing projects from consideration for a while; they are concerned about closing their project options too early. Maybe the ideas are just a little ahead of the technology. Maybe you want this project in a year or so, but not now. Whatever your reason, you don't want to forget about the project, but you don't want to have to think about it all the time. That's why you can create a parking lot for projects you don't want to actively consider but don't want to forget about. The parking lot solves the problem for people who like to cross things off their lists and for people who don't want to close their options.

Project Parking Lot

Project Name	Date Project Put on Parking Lot	Value Discussion	Notes About Project
Calendar Integration	Feb 1, 2006	If we can do this, significant value for longtime customers	Integration is not possible right now. Reevaluate when syncing with other devices works.

Parking lots make all the project portfolio decisions easier because you don't have to think about projects not in current consideration.

8.2 Conduct a Portfolio Evaluation Meeting

When you evaluate the portfolio, you'll hold a special meeting. In the past, you might have called this a *management review* or a *project status review.* Because many people have worked in organizations where management review means the dog-and-pony show for serial life cycles, I prefer to call these meetings *portfolio evaluation* meetings, because that's what they are.

You have just one goal for a portfolio evaluation meeting: to rank each project. In order to do that, you'll decide for each project whether you should commit to the project, kill the project, or transform the project in some way. You do not have a goal of solving project problems. Your job is to facilitate the decision about the project's future. That's all.

How Do You Fund Exploratory Projects?

Many organizations encourage their technical staff to work part-time on one or more current projects and work part-time on a future-direction, innovation, or skunkworks project. Working part-time is a good idea, and you need to manage it. I prefer to chunk some of the innovation work together in a timebox. Other people, such as many Googlers, like to take their 20 percent each week.

Whichever mode you prefer, don't expect people to work part-time on very different projects and make progress. You also can't tell people, "It's Tuesday at 3 p.m. Start innovating now!"

What you can do is timebox the work for the existing projects—those projects that extend the current product line. And, timebox the work for the future possible projects—those projects that may be some sort of major innovation. If you're not sure you want to spend a lot of time on future work, make those timeboxes shorter than the normal timebox. The key is to have deliverables at the end of each timebox. In the case of existing projects, the deliverables are working product chunks. In the case of future projects, the deliverables might be answers to questions, rather than a working product. See "How to Use Inch-Pebbles When You Think You Can't" (Rot99) to see how to define those deliverables. But there is no point in having people work on projects without frequent deliverables. You just can't tell how much progress they are making and whether it's worth the company's time and money to continue funding the project.

One example of timeboxing future work is what Google does with its 20 percent approach to innovation. Every engineer gets to use 20 percent of his or her time on something not specifically in his or her job description. Sometimes, people take their 20 percent time in chunks, not just one day a week, but several days per week during one week.

If innovation is important to you (and why wouldn't it be?), make sure you allow some slack in your projects. See *Slack: Getting Past Burnout, Busywork, and the Myth of Total Efficiency* (DeM01). If everyone is always full up for each timebox, they will not be able to innovate or see opportunities for innovation. And, they have no time to think. Make sure people have time to think as they proceed with their projects.

Make sure you address the issues of exploratory projects as you collaborate on and evaluate the project portfolio.

To make the decision, you need the right people at the meeting. The people who need to make the decisions are people who set the strategic direction of the organization and the people who provide the information about the project. For many organizations, that's an operating committee of some sort plus the product owner/product manager and the project manager for the projects under consideration.

Once you have the right people present, you need two pieces of project data: what the project demo looks like (can you see visible project progress?) and what the team's velocity is since the last time you had an evaluation meeting (an historical velocity chart for the project). You also need to know about project obstacles and what the organization's strategy is. I like to ask four questions at the evaluation meeting:

- Does this project still fit into our strategy? Check to see the project still fits.

- What have you finished since the last evaluation meeting? The project team provides the demo here.

- Where are you in the product backlog? The project team provides velocity and a backlog burndown chart.

- Where are your obstacles? This will tell you whether there is risk for continuing this project in the same way.

Publicize your project evaluation list so each project can prepare their information in advance. This information should come directly from what the project team already creates for their project dashboard.

If you work in an organization that tracks project cost, you'll need to also know the run rate (the cost of the project per unit time), the total project cost, and possibly the monthly/quarterly/yearly project cost data. For possible measurements, see Section 10.2, *What You Need to Measure About Your Projects*, on page 127.

Project Evaluation List
Ask these questions for each project

Does the project still fit with the overall strategy?	❏
What have you finished since the last evaluation meeting? (Be ready to demo)	❏
Where is the project with respect to backlog?	❏
What are the project's obstacles?	❏

I bet the last three questions look familiar to you. Yes, they are quite similar to a standup meeting's questions. The difference here is that you need data about the project so you can decide whether the team is making sufficient progress to continue the project. The data you need is about running, tested features. You don't need any other data.

As you consider these questions, think about which of these projects have become high-demand projects since the last time you evaluated the portfolio. A high-demand project can be one that supports the organization, grows the business, or creates new opportunities. A change in high-demand projects will change your portfolio.

Sometimes your strategy changes, especially because of outside forces. It may not matter if the project is chugging along. You still need to know whether this project is worth continuing *for now*.

If you're working in an organization that's just moving to agile, your project managers may not be accustomed to velocity charts or other ways to show progress about running, tested features. In that case, publicize your questions in advance so the project manager or the team knows the information to provide. If they can't provide enough data about what they've done and their velocity, stop the project. You can't tell whether they are making enough progress to know whether it's worth continuing to fund this project.

Yes, that's a tough stance. But if your project manager and team can't provide you with visible progress and velocity data, how can you really know whether it's worth your money and time continuing the project? Allowing them to continue the project is like a parent whose teenager uses more cell phone minutes or text messages on the plan and takes no action. If you don't make the teenager pay or at least limit the cell phone use, why would the teenager think their current behavior is unacceptable? In my experience, when the managers who review the portfolio stop a project because the project team isn't gathering data, the team initiates their first retrospective and learns what they could do to supply that data.

This is the bare outline of the portfolio evaluation meeting. Chances are good that your evaluation meetings and initial ranking meetings are not going to be easy. Read Chapter 6, *Collaborate on the Portfolio*, on page 69 for ideas on how to collaborate on the decisions you need to make.

Traffic-Light Status Reports Provide No Useful Data

Serial life-cycle projects can't provide you with the data you need for making portfolio decisions. That's because the project has no visible progress and no velocity until very late in the project. Even if you have architecture or design documents, they have little value in the lean sense of value, because the documents are not working product. For years, project managers have used traffic-light status reports: green means the project is on track, yellow means the project is at risk, and red means the project is in serious trouble.

But because a serial life-cycle project is not delivering chunks of completed work at any time, in reality the project is always red—*because you don't know its real status.* Even iterative life-cycle projects that don't finish chunks of work have the same problem. Incremental life-cycle projects can provide you with some demo data throughout the project and can provide velocity data. But only agile life cycles can guarantee you a demo and a velocity chart at the end of each timebox.

Never accept a traffic-light status report in a portfolio evaluation meeting. The traffic light provides no data for your decision.

It doesn't matter what life cycle you use: a more traditional life cycle or an agile life cycle. Every project can use these approaches assuming you manage the risks. If you use a serial life cycle, make the project small enough so the project is done by the time you reevaluate the portfolio. If the project team uses an iterative life cycle, you can see prototypes at the very least and still ask the same questions. If the project team uses an incremental life cycle, you can see features as the team completes them. You can use each life cycle type as long as you manage the risk of not being able to rank each project by keeping the projects small.

As a side effect, using data to drive portfolio decisions will help your organization become more adaptive and more agile.

8.3 Conduct a Portfolio Evaluation Meeting at Least Quarterly to Start

In Section 7.1, *Decide When to Review the Portfolio*, on page 91, I suggest some ways you can consider how often to review your project portfolio. When you're starting, review the portfolio at least once a quarter. Even if everything is perfect now—your strategy changes less frequently than once a quarter, your projects are finishing on time, your next projects start on time, you can fully staff your projects, and you can fully fund your projects—perfection is not going to last forever. You need to see the feedback the projects can provide you with for their progress and how well they continue to fit into the strategic plan.

> **Our Business Changed Almost Overnight**
> *by Wendy*, CTO
>
> We handle the communications between delivery vehicles and the main distribution point. We're tooling along, adding new features to our reporting service.
>
> We had a client/server application we'd developed back in the 90s. First we heard from one client that they wanted web-based reporting. Then another. And another. Then we learned of a potential competitor who didn't have as good a product but had the kind of reporting our customers wanted. We know we have to do this.
>
> Well, we'd done small web-based apps for use in-house. We'd never done one where our clients' private information had to be available 24/7, with security. And, I realized that if we could do this, we could expand our business dramatically. But we didn't foresee this, and we didn't know how to do it.
>
> Before we did anything, we gathered as an operations committee, looked at all our projects, and asked, "Is there a project that's a higher priority than this one?" No. We would be out of business—not today, not tomorrow, but within a few years—if we didn't do this project.
>
> That's when we decided the risk of not doing this project was higher than any return we might realize from our current projects. We finished that project, and now we have several skunkworks-type projects to explore other kinds of communications among our clients' different locations: the factories, the trucks, the distribution points, the offices.
>
> We realized we are in a different business than we thought we were. Luckily, we were able to redirect our efforts quickly. If we hadn't had a project portfolio, I don't know whether we would have known about all the projects people were working on, so we wouldn't have known how to reorganize who was working on what and when.

\\//
°ɔf **Joe Asks...**
~ <u>**Do We Run the Risk of Never Finishing Anything?**</u>

You may be concerned about evaluating the portfolio more often than once a quarter. If you change your mind about what to commit to each time you evaluate, can you ever finish anything?

Yes. And, you do have to watch how often you change your mind about the ranking.

Ask yourself this: does the value of this project change that much each time you evaluate the portfolio? In my experience, the top few projects don't change rank every time you evaluate the portfolio. Until they are done, they are still the top-ranked projects. And those are the projects that will provide the most value to you. If you do find that your top-ranked projects do change every time you evaluate the portfolio, ask yourself, "What business are we in?" and take another look at your mission. (See Chapter 11, *Define Your Mission*, on page 147.)

Normally, it's the lower-ranked projects that change their value to the organization.

There are times when you might want to evaluate the portfolio more frequently than once a quarter. If you are in a volatile market and your competitors are releasing products at least once a quarter, you want to be able to change more quickly than once a quarter. If you are new to agile and you're not sure how well the project teams are progressing, conducting a portfolio evaluation more often than once a quarter will help the teams provide data and learn about the other data they might need in order to do a great job for the projects.

I have not worked at an organization that could successfully evaluate the portfolio every six months or even less frequently without missing too many opportunities to manage which projects to commit to, to kill, or to transform. When these organizations didn't make explicit portfolio decisions, each manager (and some technical staff) made their own decisions. The organization did not have a unified approach to the portfolio. If your organization does not need the frequent evaluation, then decide how often to review the portfolio. But make an honest decision.

8.4 Review Your Decisions

As you conduct the portfolio evaluation, make sure you have a decision about each project: commit, kill, or transform. If you haven't made a decision about each and every project, you are not done.

Managing the project portfolio isn't difficult at all when you're using an agile life cycle. It's close to impossible with a waterfall, and it varies with the length of the project if you're using an iterative or incremental life cycle. If you can't use an agile life cycle, keep your projects to no more than six months in duration so you can iterate on the portfolio at least twice a year.

It might help to take a look at the decision flow.

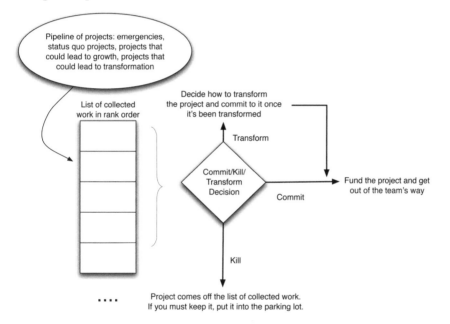

Once you're done with the evaluation part of the meeting, you can rerank the projects. You might need some of the approaches in Chapter 6, *Collaborate on the Portfolio*, on page 69.

8.5 Now Try This

- Review your collected work. Do you have everything on your list yet? If not, add it.
- Do you have any pet projects on this list? If so, do you know how to kill them?
- Do you have any doomed projects on this list? If so, can you kill them now?

Chapter 9

Evolve Your Portfolio

When you shift the focus from "project" to "running, tested features," you'll change what your project staff works on. Instead of planning for the future, they plan for the now—to get to "done," whatever that means for their project.

You'll find that the management focus changes as well. The way you use and manage your portfolio will be different. You'll begin to apply a lean approach. Lean approaches work well when you're having trouble deciding which project is number one. With lean, you don't have to know about projects; you need only to rank features.

Instead of having to manage the relative ranking of *projects*, you can manage the portfolio as a backlog of related features. All you need to know is the relative value of each feature and approximately how long it takes your team to finish a feature. Of course, you do have to do a little strategic planning all the time to make sure your vision and strategy match what you're asking the team to do. You'll find that it's easier to plan a little, do a little, check that it's all coherent, and replan than it is to have to cancel an eighteen-month project that no longer has any value. Right?

9.1 Lean Helps You Evolve Your Portfolio Approach

If you don't have to think about projects anymore, you can use lean and agile approaches to making the portfolio decisions. With the lean principles in mind, you can see that organizing work as agile projects, using pull approaches to organize the work, provides you with the maximum flexibility in managing the project portfolio.

Review your portfolio. Do you see projects that are contributing to waste, rather than removing wastes? Sometimes that waste arises from how the projects are organized. For example, if your projects are based on everyone multitasking all the time, you have tremendous waste. If you try to define all the requirements up front and implement across the architecture instead of by feature, you will have waste. If the project team does not think in terms of value and finishes the most valuable features first, you will have waste.

If you're not sure how to apply lean principles to your projects, try stabilizing something about your project work, such as the timebox, queue length, item size, or cost per feature. But you can't use a waterfall life cycle at all; a serial life cycle won't work. You may be able—with a lot of work—to modify an iterative or incremental life cycle if you keep whatever you're fixing to a very small size. But if you're going to do that, why not use an iterative/incremental or agile life cycle? Agile life cycles match lean principles. The other life cycles don't.

When you choose to stabilize something, such as the timebox, queue length, item size, or cost, you rarely need to make a big decision (Section 6.8, *Never Make a Big Commitment*, on page 79). And, you can avoid having projects. That might seem like a strange thing to say in a book about project portfolio management, but hang in here with me a minute. If you can deliver value every week or two or three or four and have a releasable product as you deliver value, the idea of a project may not make as much sense anymore. Instead of thinking about projects, you can think about releases: internal and external. If your external releases are always the same as your internal releases, you don't need to be tied to projects. Instead, you can work based on a fixed time, a fixed size of work, a fixed queue of work, or a fixed cost of work.

Deciding what to stabilize can be tricky.

9.2 Choose What to Stabilize

To decide what to stabilize, look at your work now. Are you already working in timeboxes? If not, start there. Projects using any life cycle can use timeboxes. Moving your projects to working in timeboxes is the easiest start at working to deliver small increments of value that will allow you to reassess each project fairly as you manage the portfolio.

\\// **Joe Asks...**

?ʃ
  How Does This Work for Hardware Projects?

Just as I explained in the sidebar on page 80, it's a little more difficult to make these ideas work for a product that has hardware as a piece of the released product. It's not impossible. Fixing the timebox is easy. Fixing the cost per feature is easy. You may want to conduct another portfolio review meeting just before you commit capital equipment or Non-Recurring Expense (NRE) money. But for the bulk of development, this works for hardware projects as easily as it does for software.

Once you're working in timeboxes, are your teams able to meet their commitment to what they intend to accomplish in a timebox? My experience is that until teams are allowed to work together for several iterations without changes to the timebox's content or team makeup, it's impossible for a team to accurately estimate what they can accomplish in a timebox. If your teams are having trouble meeting their timebox commitments, consider stabilizing the item size.

Once you can reduce item sizes so they are relatively small, you can move to a fixed-size queue of work. Then it won't matter what project your team is working on.

Stabilizing a feature cost requires small item sizes, because it's impossible for a team to accurately estimate large chunks of work. Short timeboxes help you fix a particular cost and help project teams predict what they can finish in a timebox.

9.3 Stabilize the Timebox

When you use an agile life cycle, you define the timebox duration at the beginning of a project. Use the same starting day and duration timebox for each team so you can decide the following at the end of each timebox (or at the end of every x timeboxes): how much value is left in continuing this project (or work or collection of features)?

You can use timeboxes in any life cycle. Timeboxes are ideally a week or two but can be as long as four weeks—any longer, and people lose the focus the timebox provides. You'll find that shorter timeboxes require little planning, certainly less than a couple of hours. You will use a sequence of timeboxes to help people build a rhythm. For more information on using timeboxes in any life cycle, see *Manage It!: Your Guide to Modern Pragmatic Project Management* [Rot07].

If you move an entire organization to working in timeboxes to decide when to release, make sure the teams meet these conditions:

- Know what "done" means for each feature. Teams cannot predict and measure velocity if they don't define "done" for each feature.

- Every team must have running, tested features at the end of every timebox. If a team can't complete some specific independent feature in a timebox, that might be OK. It's not OK if they break the product. At the end of every timebox, the product must be releasable. That allows the project team to have a stopping point, which mentally frees them to work on the most valuable project next, whether it is this one or not.

- Management and the product owners must agree on a minimal set of releasable features. If management and product owners don't agree, you will never release a product to your customers. Well, you will when some senior manager yells, "Ship the damned thing already," but that's not a *planned* release.

- Timeboxes must be short enough so a team doesn't fall out of its rhythm (see *Manage It!* [Rot07]). That's a timebox of no more than four weeks. If a team loses its rhythm, it ceases to be productive. Just because you have a timebox does not mean the team will maintain its velocity.

9.3.1 When You Can't Stabilize the Timebox

If you have to integrate software or hardware from someone else and they are not accustomed to working in timeboxes, you may not be sure how to maintain your timeboxes. In that circumstance, you might be able to maintain a timebox for your work, but not work for the entire product. For example, at the beginning of a timebox, you might assign some tasks that say "Work with drop from vendor" without a specific size attached to it. In addition, you may have to change your definition of what "done" means for the end of a timebox.

I can't think of another reason to not be able to maintain a timebox. If the technical staff overcommit to work and can't finish all of it in a timebox, reduce the duration of the timebox so that they can learn to estimate how much work they can do in a shorter period of time.

9.4 Stabilize the Number of Work Items in Progress

Fixing the work size means fixing the amount of work in progress. That can work on two levels: the number of tasks in process for a given project, what I'll call *kanban-in-the-small*, and the number of projects in process, what I'll call *kanban-in-the-large*.

Kanban is a system of seeing the work in progress and knowing when it's time to put more work items in the queue to be worked on. Kanban literally means a signboard, as in *Toyota Production System* [Ohn88]. The team can see the work in progress—one feature and the work yet to do, all on one board.

For example, in all serial life-cycle projects, you have a list of features. Most iterative and incremental life-cycle projects have a similar long list of features. That feature list changes and tends to grow the longer the project is. In agile projects, there is a product backlog that is reranked for each timebox, and the team takes the next chunk of what they think they can complete off the backlog.

One of the best ways to make kanban systems work is to think of each entry in a product backlog as its own minimum marketable feature (MMF); see *Software by Numbers: Low-Risk, High-Return Development* [DCH03]. A project team works on just one thing—a minimum marketable feature—until that MMF is complete. When that MMF is complete, the team can release the product.

Why is an MMF so important? It's because that's the basis of project portfolio management. Projects don't matter; the set of MMFs you are ready to release is what your customers buy, as we discussed earlier. A completed MMF provides value to the organization.

When a team uses a kanban system, the team limits the number of tasks in progress at any time. At Agile 2007, Arlo Belshee described what he called *naked planning*,[1] a way to limit what the team sees to no more than seven MMFs. The team works on one MMF at a time. There is no minimum or maximum feature size, but the customer who

---

1. See http://joearnold.com/2008/03/naked-planning-kanban-simplified/ for a video brief description of some of Arlo's informal talks at Agile 2007.

requests the feature tends to ask for smaller features to limit the time the team is unavailable to work on new features.

You don't need to have a queue of just seven items as Arlo describes. Your queue can be any size. The key with kanban is that enough people work on one MMF and *complete* it before taking another feature of the queue.

With kanban systems, your project team can even work on multiple MMFs as long as the team can release the product once one MMF is complete. This means the team has to have great source control so the team can work on multiple MMFs and still be able to release as soon as one MMF is complete.

To use kanban effectively, the team must keep a sustainable pace, and someone (or some defined set of people) decides what the ranking of each waiting item is. But, the team doesn't care what they work on. They just take the next item off the list. That's why you can use kanban for projects as a whole to manage the whole portfolio and for a given project to manage when you complete each feature.

9.4.1 Fix the Number of Tasks In-Process, Kanban-in-the-Small

One way to avoid projects but still manage the portfolio is to stabilize the number of feature sets in process. Here you can see that one feature set, a minimally marketable feature set, is in progress. That feature set has seven tasks. Of those seven, four have not yet been started, two are in progress, and one is done. Once all the tasks are complete, the team can release the MMF.

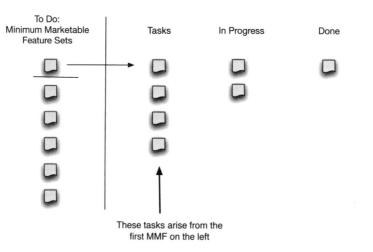

These tasks arise from the
first MMF on the left

When you stabilize the number of in-process tasks, especially if you are able to define a minimum marketable feature set as a relatively small number of tasks, you see a number of benefits. With so few in-process tasks, people actively work together to complete tasks.

- Projects complete faster because there's no (or at least much less) wasted work.

- Because you're implementing by feature, the team and you can see the project's progress easily.

9.4.2 Fix the Number of Projects In-Process, Kanban-in-the-Large

Some management teams, even when they've ranked the portfolio, have a difficult time assigning teams to just one project until that project is complete. But aside from the benefits to the team of avoiding multi-tasking, you receive a ton of benefits by fixing the number of projects underway:

- You know you are never going to starve a project of its necessary people. That's because you never assign more projects than you have teams.

- The teams all learn all the projects. You don't have to worry about cross-training, because the idea of specializing in types of projects goes away.

- Developers (or testers or writers or whomever) never have to worry about projects that are like albatrosses. That's because the *team* has responsibility for the project, not management. And, the team may not be assigned to this project each time a particular product needs more work.

- Projects complete faster because there's no competition from other projects.

- It's easy to organize your project portfolio, because you and the organization's leaders define what the organization needs to work on *now* and what can be postponed until the next evaluation.

Any project with any life cycle can use a kanban queue. It might look different depending on your life cycle. In the picture on the following page, you can see how an organization that wants three projects in process for one team has queue limits on what's ready to start (seven items), what can be in the development and review queue (four items), what can be in test (three), and what can be in final review (one).

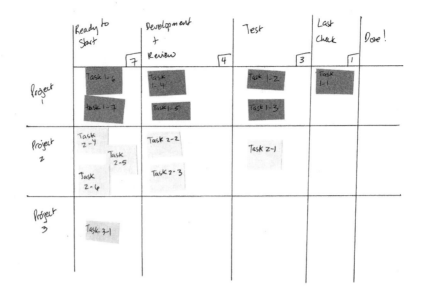

Kanban for software, whether you apply it to a portfolio or to a single project, has this requirement: all of the items in the queue, the MMFs, must be roughly the same size.

The MMFs must be something the team can complete in a relatively short period of time, because there is no timebox to maintain the team's rhythm. Instead, the team's rhythm arises from completing work.

This approach to the project portfolio requires significant discipline from every manager in the organization. As soon as one person tries to push his or her project ahead of another or ask a technical person to multitask, kanban-in-the-large falls apart.

9.4.3 When You Can't Fix the Work Size

Some projects have an ebb and flow. Some teams have to account for maintenance work or other product support work in their projects. You can still use kanban. As the team completes one MMF, they take their next chunk of work from the queue labeled "Urgent", for example.

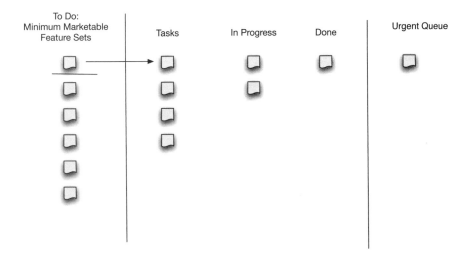

Kanban is great for managing a large queue of defects, especially if it's easy to release the product after each fix. But kanban is not easy to implement for many teams.

In order to stabilize the amount of work in progress, you have to become accomplished at defining MMFs of roughly the same size. But, many product owners, product managers, and product development teams are not good at estimating the relative size of feature sets. If you're working on a new, never-been-done-before product, you have never worked in timeboxes, and the team has never tried to estimate separating size from duration, then you may have trouble with kanban. In addition, if your team has few generalists and many specialists, it will be difficult to work on just one MMF at one time.

To fix the queue size for a project, the team needs to create small MMFs of similar size. To fix the queue size for a portfolio, the team needs to be able to work on any product, and the people ranking the requirements need to define MMFs of relatively small size. If your organization can't do that, you won't be able to stabilize the work queue.

9.5 Fix the Queue Length for a Team

A related option to fixing the number of in-process tasks for a project is to fix the number of in-process tasks for a team. Each task takes as long as it takes—although this works well when you have relatively smaller tasks and works less well as the task size increases.

At Agile 2007, Arlo Belshee discussed the idea of what he called a *Disneyland queue*. With a fixed-length queue (he uses a queue of seven items) and historical velocity, the team estimates a "your time from here" estimate for the last item in the queue:

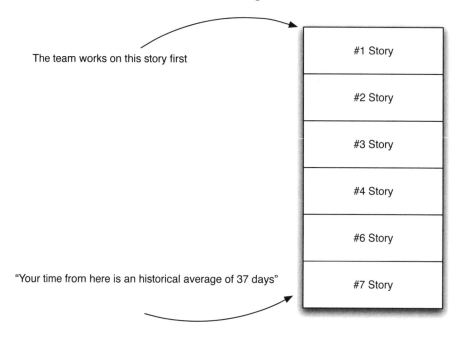

Note that the team doesn't estimate each item in the queue. The product owner, customer, product manager—whoever is in charge of ranking requirements—is the one who has some idea of how big each item is and, more important, how valuable each item is. The team doesn't estimate the item until they start it.

Of course, if they realize this item is much bigger than other items, they let the product owner know. The product owner can then work with the team to break down the large task into smaller user stories. The product owner reranks all the user stories. Then, the entire team works on the first item in the queue until it's done, as in releasable. Then, the team takes the next item off the queue to work on together.

Not all items need the entire team. In that case, the first item takes all precedence, and as team members are available, they work on the next item. This is a similar team assignment as in Section 5.2, *Rank Order the Projects in the Portfolio Using Points*, on page 48, except that here, the team is assigned to one task in the queue, not a whole project.

9.5.1 When You Can't Fix the Queue Length

Fixing the queue length is great for organizations and teams that are accustomed to working in a rhythm and in small chunks. If your team or your management is not accustomed to implementing by feature or a rhythm to the projects, you are not going to be able to fix the queue length. Not only will your management have to make a binary decision about which feature is done next, the feature size has to stay small.

Stabilizing the queue length requires substantial discipline from everyone: the product owner, the management, and the technical staff.

9.6 When You Need to Fix Cost

Well-meaning people have used waterfall life cycles as a way to control costs. They thought that if they monitored the documents throughout the life cycle, the documents would have some relationship to the product. We know that to be untrue. But serial life cycles persisted, and many managers derive (undeserved) comfort from them.

One of the big problems in a waterfall project is that you can't make the decision to kill or change the project until very late in the project's life cycle. So, when you need to fix cost, you want a life cycle that allows you as much flexibility making cost decisions as possible. That means agile.

If you need to work on a fixed-price contract, have the customer rank the requirements, explain how velocity works, and show the same kinds of data as you would in a portfolio evaluation review (see Section 8.2, *Conduct a Portfolio Evaluation Meeting*, on page 104). Now, you as the development group, work in a rhythm to finish as much of the work as possible. Your best bet is to fix a timebox of no more than two weeks, as in Section 9.3, *Stabilize the Timebox*, on page 115.

9.7 Management Changes When You Stabilize Something About Your Projects

Fixing something about your projects has a sobering effect on management. Once you've made the decision to fix a timebox, you can't change it. You can't reduce or increase the timebox duration without creating obstacles for the team, because you've destroyed their velocity as well as removed their ability to measure it. You can't ask people to put in overtime for the same reason. Once you've prevented a team from measuring their velocity, they have no idea where they are, and neither do you. You can't ask for multitasking either. You can't keep arbitrarily large projects in the pipeline without breaking them down into their component parts of feature set chunks. (Not architectural components, smaller sets of features.)

What you get is management "discipline." It's the discipline to manage for results (as in *Managing for Results* [Dru64]), not for activities. It's the discipline to make a decision and keep it, as long as it still fits the strategy. It is wonderful. But you have to be a disciplined manager to do this.

Not only do you get management discipline, you also get team discipline to focus on one thing at a time until it's done.

9.8 Now Try This

- Review your portfolio. Do you see projects that are contributing to waste, rather than removing wastes?

- What can you stabilize about your projects? Is it possible to fix the size of the queue of tasks? Or the size of the items in the queue?

- Have you or other managers resisted stabilizing something about your projects? Write down why that works for you.

- If you've tried this, what kinds of management costs have you seen?

Chapter 10

Measure the Essentials

You could try any number of measures to evaluate your projects: cost, duration, earned value, and consumer ROI, to name a few. But these measurements alone don't provide you with a useful measure of how much value the project is contributing or could contribute to the organization. You want to measure enough about projects to know whether they are running smoothly so you can make the commit/kill/transform decision. And, you need to know whether the project is still returning value to the organization to know whether you should commit to the next set of features for the project.

Your measurements help you know whether the project is returning value to the organization. They tell you how smoothly the project is running. And, they can provide a baseline for seeing change. In this chapter, we will consider possible measures that will help you know whether a project is making progress and the value it provides to the organization.

10.1 Measure Value

As a leader in the organization, you care about the number of projects successfully completed per unit time.[1] Projects that don't successfully complete lead to emergency projects, which reduces your management effectiveness and your ability to provide value to the organization, as in Figure 2.2, on page 11. When teams take a long time to complete

---

1. Yes, this is a measure that can be gamed. All you need to do is make the projects smaller, and you have more projects completed per unit time.

projects, you don't enough flexibility to change what's going on in the organization—to actually manage the project portfolio.

Be careful when measuring project completion time. It is just a surrogate measurement for what you really want to measure—a continuous value stream. A project is what you decide it is. Remember, customers don't buy or use projects—they buy sets of running, tested features. If you really want to measure projects, go ahead. I won't stop you. It might help you see how short you can make your projects and be successful. But you can't normalize projects against each other to compare their value to the organization. I find measuring projects makes managing the portfolio more complex than it has to be. Instead, I recommend you measure the time it takes a team to complete a set running, tested features (Section 10.2, *What You Need to Measure About Your Projects*, on the next page) so you can manage the project portfolio effectively.

If you're stuck in a serial life cycle such as phase-gate or waterfall and can't measure running, tested features, consider changing your approach to product development. If you manage the portfolio, reviewing the progress made on running, tested features by your teams, you don't need a serial life cycle, because you don't need the early milestones to attempt to gauge progress. Using an agile life cycle provides the most information early, but even choosing an iterative life cycle to try some prototypes at the beginning of a project, followed by building the product incrementally, will still provide you with more information than a serial life cycle. For more information about life cycles and how to combine them, see *Manage It!* [Rot07] and "What Lifecycle? Selecting the Right Model for Your Project" [Rot08b].

If you really can't move to agile or incremental approaches for your projects, you will have to rely on the old, traditional measures, such as ROI. Read *Developing Products in Half the Time: New Rules, New Tools* [SR98] or the financial measures section of *Agile Estimating and Planning* [Coh06]. You will spend a huge amount of management time defining and gathering these measures. And, because you're not using incremental or agile approaches, you won't be able to adapt to what's going on in the world. In reality, your measurements will not provide you with the information you need to *manage* the project portfolio. You will be guessing.

By now, I hope you've used any of the approaches in Chapter 5, *Rank the Portfolio*, on page 47 to rank your portfolio. If you're ready to take advantage of all the ways you can use the portfolio—to trade off between projects, to stop projects when they are done enough, and to schedule the next projects—you might need additional measurements to see whether the projects are returning some value. You'll need some project and some portfolio measurements.

10.2 What You Need to Measure About Your Projects

For projects, you need to measure the completion of running, tested features over time (as in *Extreme Programming Installed* [JAH02]), in other words, the team's velocity over time. That's all you need to measure—assuming your measures are correct. If your team doesn't actually finish features, as in done-done-done, you will need other measurements, such as defects and schedule dates.

When I say done-done-done, I mean that the product is working and documented enough that a customer could use it. The code is checked in, the developers and testers have planned and run "enough" tests, the documentation exists and is correct, any hardware is working, and the code has passed enough testing that the project team has confidence in it and the product is releasable for a customer to use.

You don't need to measure the number of defects, although knowing those will help you determine whether this project is sufficiently valuable as is. You don't need to measure start and end dates, although you may want this data for organizing the portfolio. You need to know how much this team can churn out in a given time period. I wish I could tell you that you could compare two teams' velocities and know which one was more productive. Sorry, comparing teams, especially those working on different projects, is like comparing oranges to frogs. The projects the team work on, how the team estimates, the environment in which the teams work, and how frequently the team has to work toward norming (as in "Stages of small group development revisited" [WJ77]) are all factors that prevent you from comparing teams.

Although it's tempting to measure projects completed per unit time, measuring that is a surrogate for the true measurement of what your users and customers want from you—completed features that work. For a lean or agile approach to managing the portfolio, consider these measures:

- The team's velocity of running, tested features and the historical velocity chart (team capacity over time).

> \\// Joe Asks...
> `?-`
> ~ **Can the Team Game These Measures?**
>
> Sure they can. Any gaming (manipulating the measures to report what they think you want as opposed to real progress) is based on management's approach to measures.
>
> If you ask teams to measure and you ask out of helpfulness and curiosity, the teams will respond with answers.
>
> As soon as you use measures to attempt to evaluate the team, try to compare two teams, punish the team, or consider layoffs based on team velocity, the team will game the measures. They will obfuscate their progress in ways that may astonish you.
>
> You have the most control over the team and their reaction to measures. Use that power to build transparency around the project portfolio and to help the team recognize and remove obstacles. Otherwise, the team will retaliate, and you will have no basis to evaluate the portfolio. You'll be back to your gut. Guts are unreliable.

- The amount of work in progress. The more work in progress, the less lean you can be.

- Obstacles preventing the team from moving faster, such as defects, insufficient automation, and incomplete stories. Obstacles are risks to the project and tend to be examples of technical debt.

- Product backlog burndown chart so you can see where in the product backlog the project is.

- If you measure cost, cost of the project since the last portfolio evaluation and the total project cost to date.

Because these are all project measures, you need to be careful about what and how you ask the team to measure themselves. Make sure you ask from a position of helpfulness and curiosity. If you use these measures to beat the team or punish them, they will game the measures in any way they can. That will prevent you from making good portfolio decisions.

Whatever measures the project teams choose, they should use a Big Visible Chart. At the very least, request velocity or some measure of work in progress on that chart.

10.3 Measure Project Velocity: Current and Historical

Since you need to know what progress the team has made since the previous portfolio evaluation, you need to see current velocity and historical velocity. If your project team has been working in the rhythm of a timebox for a number of iterations, understands how to break down requirements into small user stories, and knows what "done" means, their velocity might look like this:

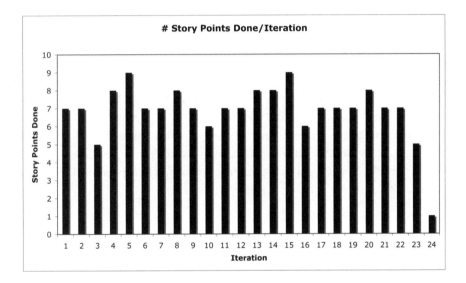

Velocity of user stories or points per iteration is an important measure, but it doesn't paint the whole picture. You also need to see how many stories are being added to the backlog. If the product owner is continually adding many items to the backlog for this project, you need to reassess the size or the strategic importance of the project.[2]

Here, the backlog growth is small over the project. The team continues to make progress. There is no issue with this project, as long it remains strategically important.

---

2. Frequent additions to the backlog could also indicate that the product owner doesn't understand the purpose of a backlog for a release.

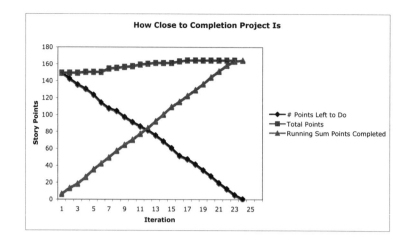

Teams who are newer to agile will need a few iterations until their velocity becomes regular. The first three iterations tend to be random and not predictable of future velocity. And, given that people are just learning how to break features into relatively smaller stories and how to define "done" for their projects, it may take even longer than three iterations—I've seen teams take nine or ten iterations—until you have a velocity that helps you predict the future. However, even unpredictable velocity helps you see what the team has accomplished, so it can be a valuable measurement. Just be careful of using it as a perfect predictor of future progress. There is no perfect predictor.

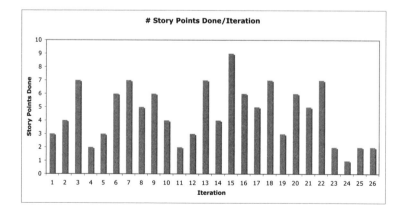

When the team has an unpredictable velocity, you will see the effect in the backlog completion chart. You can see in this next figure that this team required a few extra iterations to finish the project, because they had an erratic velocity. But even with an unpredictable velocity, you would still have data to evaluate the project's progress, especially if you also saw a product demo.

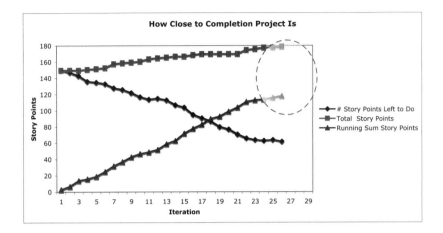

If your team is having trouble using velocity as a predictor, make sure no one is adding new stories to an iteration underway, and encourage the team to report other obstacles so you can see whether technical debt is preventing them from making a more predictable progress. Ask the team to report how much work in progress they have, as in Section 10.4, *Measure Cumulative Flow for the Project*, on the next page. And, make sure the team is not using a serial life cycle. You can see the results for this team that started using a serial life cycle for a few iterations:

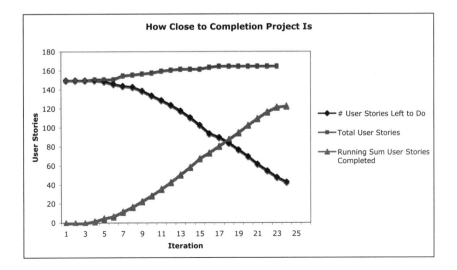

The team decided they needed several architectural iterations at the beginning of the project. The manager explained that without visible progress, the project would be canceled. (PowerPoint architecture, as defined in *Practices of an Agile Developer: Working in the Real World* [SH06], was not visible progress.) The team decided it was time to finish a few features, starting in the fourth iteration.

You might hear team members say, "We have to get the architecture/ infrastructure right before we start." Teams who are new to agile do believe this—you might, too. But, my experience with agile teams, and other people's experience with agile teams who use collective code ownership, has found that you *can* grow the architecture or infrastructure as you proceed building features. See *Manage It!* and *Extreme Programming Explained* [Bec00] for suggestions on how to start a project without a lot of architecture work up front, and see *Refactoring: Improving the Design of Existing Code* [FBB+99] and *Refactoring to Patterns* [Ker04] for how to evolve the architecture as you proceed. You might need some time to evaluate the architecture. But you don't need an entire iteration devoted to architecture. Your project will turn into a serial life-cycle project, which makes it difficult to evaluate in a regular short time period as part of a portfolio.

But what happens when a project doesn't show any velocity at all for several iterations? That's when you must ask questions in your portfolio evaluation meeting about the project, about its strategic importance, and about whether the project is possible to finish. And, it's time to measure work in progress. Instead of finishing features, your team may have substantial work in progress. That doesn't provide value to the organization and may be invisible to the team.

10.4 Measure Cumulative Flow for the Project

Cumulative flow is a measure of the work in progress over time compared to the total project scope. Many agile teams measure cumulative flow to see whether they are starting more work than they can finish in an iteration.

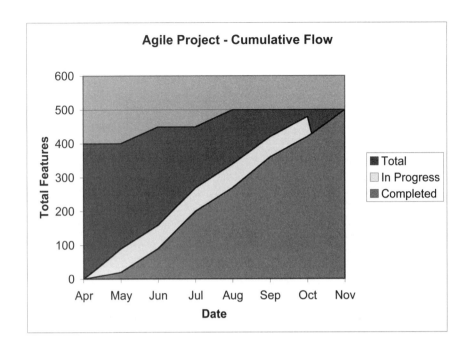

The value to the team of measuring cumulative flow is the team can see whether they need to start fewer features and "swarm" around them to complete them earlier. For you, the one evaluating the project portfolio, the value is in seeing how much work in progress there is. The more work in progress, the less this project has provided value to the organization.

When you start managing the project portfolio, consider asking all your project teams to measure cumulative flow and report it during the portfolio evaluation meeting. If you have teams who are not using agile approaches, you and they need to know whether they have a lot of work in progress and whether you can make any predictions about when that work could be done.

Cumulative flow shows you the work in progress and how long that work in progress takes. You can see that a serial life-cycle project has significantly more work in progress than the agile team does. In fact, the completed work looks like a hockey stick: a flat line at the beginning and a rapid increase in finishing at the end. Iterative or incremental life cycles have less work in progress.

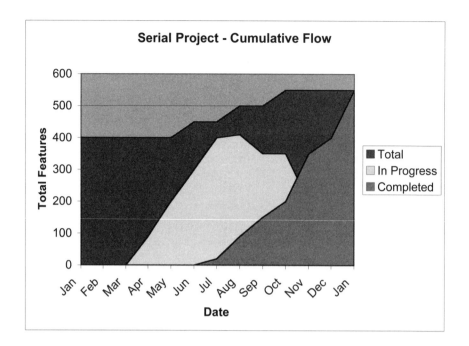

It's useful to consider cumulative flow when you have to consider which projects will provide the most value fastest. Measuring cumulative flow provides this value to you:

- The project teams can see their progress. Instead of keeping work in progress invisible, now the team can see it.

- The project team may start to use lean and agile approaches themselves to make more progress.

- You can take a leaner approach to the project portfolio, as in Section 2.4, *Lean Approaches to the Project Portfolio*, on page 14, which will allow you to complete projects faster.

10.5 Measure Obstacles Preventing the Team's Progress

Sometimes, a team has a zero or low velocity because of obstacles that prevent them from delivering running, tested features. In that case, ask the team to measure those obstacles.

Measuring obstacles might seem like a strange thing to measure. "JR, I don't have space for a standup meeting. How that heck do I measure that?" But you can measure obstacles. If you've asked for space for a standup and you can't get it, you list the obstacle and how long it has been since you asked for space.

Obstacle Report

Rank	Obstacle	Request Date	Days Since Request Date
1	Chair for Jim	Feb 1	15
2	Need tester full time	Jan 1	44
3	Standup meeting area with whiteboard	Jan 7	38

Any time a project team doesn't get the resources it needs, it won't be able to deliver the value your managers thought it would when you ranked it in the project portfolio. If you track a top-ten risk list, you could use that as your obstacle report.

Project managers: don't put more than ten obstacles on your report. You will overwhelm your leadership team, and they will either ignore you or try to solve those problems in the portfolio evaluation meeting. You want your sponsor or someone from the leadership team to work with you to remove obstacles. Ask for help outside of the project portfolio evaluation meeting. Leadership team: if you see an obstacle report with more than ten obstacles, you have a team in trouble. Pay attention to them. They need help. Get them what they need.

But the more interesting obstacles are the ones measuring technical debt. Those can be defects, a lack of automated tests, or product-based technical debt. For defect charts, see the charts in *Manage It!* [Rot07]. This technical debt chart might be a way to show other technical debt in the product. You might see evidence of technical debt in the speed and frequency in which the project team finishes stories.

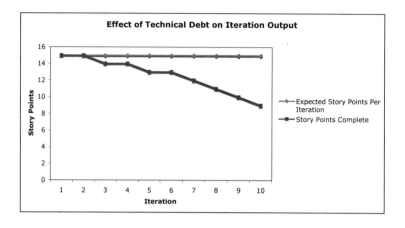

Once people can see that the project team is working more slowly because of technical debt, you can put a dollar amount on it, which you can use to decide whether paying off technical debt is worth more than some new features.

Here, the project team is not keeping up with the expected number of automated tests, leaving a debt for this iteration of thirty-four automated tests. Is that a big number? I can't tell. Maybe it's a business decision. Maybe they estimated wrong. Maybe they need those tests, and they are going to have trouble in a future iteration. Right now, you can't tell anything from the data, except that it's time to ask more questions.

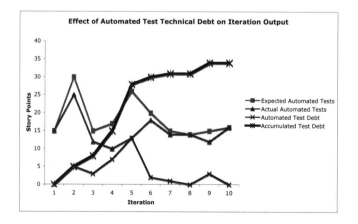

In this case, the technical debt is caused by a lack of some automated tests and a lack of redesign of older code. The technical team wants to add some automated tests, but the product owner wants more features.

(Yes, some agile teams leave *all* product backlog decisions to the product owner.) Once the product owner sees that the team is capable of supplying only about two-thirds of the story points for the same time, the product owner is more likely to change the items in the product backlog to include more technical debt items. But if the product owner doesn't, management can.

As a different example, in the following figure the team has an initial zero velocity in the iteration—they finish zero stories until the last week of an iteration. Not all teams finish stories at the same frequency throughout an iteration. But not finishing *any* stories until the last week of the iteration is an indication of a problem and could be technical debt. There are other reasons, such as too much work in progress or that the team is using a too-serial approach inside the iteration. Using a chart like this one is a way of making the problem transparent so the team can do something about it.

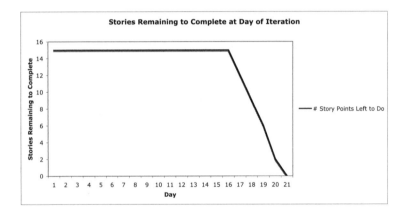

If you're working on a legacy product where you know you have technical debt, the earlier you can measure it, the easier it will be to address the debt in the backlog or in the project portfolio ranking and, by inference, how many people are assigned to the project. If you're working on a project team that's new to agile, you might want to measure technical debt so you aren't surprised by what "done" means. And, if you're on an experienced agile team, you can prevent waste in the organization by being proactive about looking for and paying off technical debt.

If you need some other ideas about how to measure technical debt, consider the following: the percentage of automated test code coverage for each feature set, a McCabe's metric for each of the highly complex modules and the time it takes to make any change in those modules, and how quickly the team completes stories inside an iteration. A number of static analysis tools can help you discover what's going on in the code. You might find there are other measures you want to take; these are just examples.

However the project team decides to show their obstacles, make sure you ask about them. Their obstacles will prevent them from making progress and may require more people or more time for the project, which might change its rank in the portfolio.

10.6 Measure the Product Backlog Burndown Chart

Sometimes the management team needs to see just how far along this project is; they might need to know not just knowing the numbers of running, tested features but also which running, tested features are complete. That's where you can generate a product backlog burndown chart.

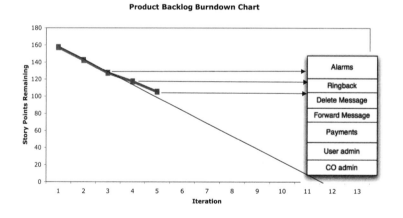

You can see that the team is not quite on their projected velocity, so it's helpful to see what has been done and what's left to do.

10.7 Measure Run Rate and Other Cost Data, If Necessary

If you're working on a fixed-price contract or working on some enhancements until the funding runs out, measure the project cost however your organization does that.

You may need to measure the "run rate" for your project, which is the iteration's or other period's fixed-price costs. If you have ten project staff members and they have an average salary of $10,000 per month, your project's monthly run rate is $100,000.

If you fund projects incrementally, as in Section 6.7, *Fund Projects Incrementally*, on page 78, you need to know your run rate so you can ask for more money when you need it.

10.8 Don't Even Try to Measure Individual Productivity

Since I've been working in the field, my managers and clients have been trying to measure productivity. What a waste. Individual productivity means nothing.

What does mean something is a team's throughput. That's right—a team. A team produces a set of running, tested features—or not. When a team produces a document, that team might be getting ready to be productive, but they haven't produced anything you can count— unless that document is required as part of the deliverable. Only when a team produces a working demo or prototype—or, even better, a working product—can you see what their productivity is.

If you try to measure individual productivity, you will get some data. And, the people whom you are measuring will game the data, have no fear. If you measure code, they'll write a ton. If you measure tests, they'll write a bazillion. If you measure files, they will have many more than the project needs. No matter what you measure, if it's not running, tested features, then they will game the system. Don't do it.

But, you say, I have several single-person projects. Surely I can measure that person's productivity. Um, no, you can't. First, I doubt that those people resist talking to each other. Second, how will you compare productivity? If Davey gets the easy projects and Sally gets the hard ones, who is more productive? I can't tell, and neither can you. Stop trying.

Single-Person Projects Aren't
by Drew, Senior Developer

I worked on a project several years ago that my boss thought was a one-man project—and I was that man. It wasn't hard, but it had a few complexities I thought I would have trouble with, so I asked a colleague, Jack, to review my code.

He did review it and gave me a bunch of suggestions. I ended up taking most of them. But when he went to fill out his time card, he was told he hadn't worked on my project. I went to see our manager.

"Look, I couldn't have done this without Jack. His review really helped me make progress."

"But this was a one-man project. Why didn't you just do it?"

"Because working with someone else for a couple of hours saved me several days. Didn't you want me to make progress quickly?"

My manager never again thought we had one-person projects.

Knowledge workers do not work in a vacuum. Some people facilitate meetings. Some people develop. Some test. Some help others see what the product manager meant in that requirement. Measuring individual productivity will encourage people to work alone and to game the system. Don't do it.

Measure a team's capacity in terms of running, tested features. Don't bother with attempting to measure productivity or efficiency. You'll make everyone frustrated (including you), and you won't get the results you want.

10.9 What You Need to Measure About the Portfolio

When you start gathering data to help your portfolio decisions, as in Section 4.2, *Decide to Commit, Kill, or Transform the Project*, on page 34, you might be able to more easily make a decision quickly. When the project teams know they will have to produce this data, they may be able to help you make the decisions too. I recommend you start with just the project portfolio burndown chart.

Remember, just as you can't calculate ROI for a project as in Section 5.9, *Don't Use ROI to Rank*, on page 63, you can't calculate ROI for the portfolio. But if you use a lean approach for the portfolio and an agile or lean approach for your projects, you don't have to try. You'll see value, or lack thereof, every time you evaluate the portfolio and can make the small adjustments you need for the organization.

In addition to the project portfolio burndown, you might need to track other data for your organization.

- Number of iterations completed, cost per iteration, total cost for the project to date

- Capital expenses for the project

- When you can capitalize software

- Number of simultaneous projects you are asking teams to work on

10.9.1 Expensing vs. Capitalizing Software

I'm not a lawyer, nor am I an accountant. You should talk to your legal and financial people to hear what they have to say, especially if your government mucks around with the issues of expensing or capitalizing software.

If you're not familiar with these terms, here's what they mean. Expensing software means you pay for the cost of the product as you develop it. The expense comes out of the organization's cash flow and off the income statement. Expensing has an immediate effect on the organization's profit and loss statement. When you pay for software as an expense, it means that the software has no inherent value as an asset to the organization.

Capitalization is different. As the software is developed, some part of it is considered an "asset" to the organization, not just an expense. Because it's an asset, it's expected to provide a greater value when it is sold than the value it currently has. If you were making a table, the cost of the wood is an expense. But at some point, as you make the legs and the top *and* put it together, the table has more value than the cost of the wood or the workers' pay to make that table. The table is an asset and can be sold at a higher value than the expenses. It's the same idea with software.

If you always generate running, tested features, you are creating an asset. I don't know when your software is an asset that you can capitalize. You, your lawyers, and your accountants are the only people who can decide that. But if you are tight on cash flow, make sure you know when you have to start counting your software development as an asset, because that may change when you need to finish a project.

10.9.2 How Many Simultaneous Projects Are You Asking a Team to Work On?

If the answer to this question is greater than one, you'd better have a good reason. Once teams attempt to work on more than one project at a time, they make less progress on all projects. That puts you in a position of not being able to manage the portfolio, being in a position

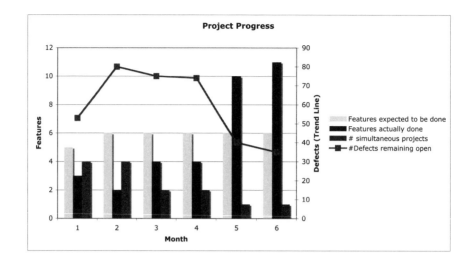

Figure 10.1: PROJECT PROGRESS, REDUCING AND ELIMINATING MULTI-TASKING

like Figure 2.2, on page 11 instead of being in a position where you are managing the portfolio, as in Figure 2.1, on page 10.

But what if you're transitioning to agile and lean approaches and you don't see another way out of the current mess you're in? What if you've decided that instead of one- or two-week iterations on just one project, you are willing to staff the team to two projects for four weeks? If you track the number of simultaneous projects the team is working on and track their velocity and technical debt, you might be surprised.

Early in my management career, I thought that asking a team to work on "just" two projects was a good idea. After all, I'd stopped having everyone work on four projects. I must be doing a good job, right? The people were working in cross-functional feature-based teams, so they had everyone they needed to finish the work. They were using continuous integration. I did see a little improvement in the first month (see Figure 10.1). But notice how much more improvement there was, not just in the number of features but in the reduction of defects, when I finally told the teams to work on just one project.

> ### How to Create a Chart Displaying Multiple Types of Data
>
> If you've never tried to create this kind of a chart in Excel, here's how. Make the bar chart line. Now, select the data you want to add as a trend line. Select the chart and "paste special." Bring up the contextual menu with a Ctrl-click or right-click depending on your machine, and you can select the trend line format.
>
> In Numbers, you can select a "mixed chart" type and follow the instructions.

10.10 Measure Capacity by Team, Not by Individual

We've all seen the differences in individual people's capabilities. If you look in the literature, you can see that *Peopleware* [DL99], *Rapid Development* [McC96], and *Psychology of Computer Programming* [Wei98] all cite differences in capabilities ranging from as little as 10:1 to as much as 100:1—that means that one developer could be as much as 100 times more productive than another.

The problem is that development is actually a small piece of what happens in a well-running team. The team has ways to discuss and resolve problems, test as individuals and as a group, help the technical support staff, interact with the rest of the organization, and perform any other team roles they need. Development, especially as an individual, is certainly necessary to completing features and projects, but it's not the only activity a healthy team undertakes. If you have only great developers, but they can't talk to the users, they can't test what they're developing, or they have no patience for the tech support folks, then you don't have a sustainable organization. You certainly don't have a productive one or one that can produce releasable running, tested features.

The only capacity measurement that makes sense is that of completed projects over time. Measuring completed projects can be useful but still has outside dependencies, such as when your customers are willing to take the release. If you want to measure capacity, measure how long it takes a team to create a running, tested feature. That way, you've accounted for the DBA time, for the testing time, for the analysis and architectural time, and for actual coding time.

10.11   People Finish More with Lean and Agile

As you're measuring project value and making progress on your project portfolio, you might notice the following phenomenon: your staff finishes more features, your projects finish earlier, and you have fewer emergencies as you integrate agile approaches and lean thinking into your projects.

Because people focus on one project at a time, complete the most valuable features first, and complete features for every timebox, project teams build their capacity. And, as managers use lean and agile approaches for the project portfolio, they need fewer teams on large programs, and they finish projects and programs faster.

I've seen two big reasons for building capacity:

- Teams have either dramatically reduced or eliminated multitasking.

- Teams require many fewer specialists to finish their work.

When a team moves to working on one project at a time, finishing valuable work in a timebox, that creates a reinforcing loop in the organization. Because that team is finishing work, the pressure to start another project drops. The team can finish more work. Once the team establishes and maintains its velocity—proving they can finish work—the organization stops piling work on simultaneously. It's much easier for the team to push back to all of the people who want work done and ask them which project or feature (as in Section 9.4, *Stabilize the Number of Work Items in Progress*, on page 117) is most important.

If you have a team that works together to accomplish completed pieces of work, you won't have quite as many problems as "Dan is the only database admin, so we have to wait for him to make us a database." Other people will work with Dan, and he will teach them the basics of what he knows. Dan might be the only person who knows how to test in a certain way or upgrade a schema or work with that part of the code base. But if you have a team of people as defined in *Behind Closed Doors* [RD05]—in other words—people who have interdependent deliverables, they will find ways to help each other accomplish the team's work. If you measure team velocity, as in Section 10.2, *What You Need to Measure About Your Projects*, on page 127, you encourage people to become generalists rather than specialists.

You won't see these benefits if you change the makeup of the team from iteration to iteration. That's because you're not letting the team form. And, there is a limit to the capacity that people can increase. But limiting work in progress at the portfolio and at the team level helps build capacity.

10.12 Now Try This

- As you decide what to measure, consider what you need from the project and what you need to measure about the portfolio.

- What will it take for your projects to report these measures?

- What will you need to do to collect the portfolio measures?

- What do you need to measure about your projects and your portfolio?

- How will you present the data or ask the team to present their data?

Chapter 11

Define Your Mission

My publisher, the Pragmatic Bookshelf, has a mission: "Make developers' lives better." They use their mission to decide whether a book proposal fits and to decide how to market and sell their intellectual property: books, workshops, podcasts, and the other products. Historically, Google's mission was "Don't be evil," but that has now evolved to "Organize the world's information and make it universally accessible and useful."[1]

Portfolio management is all about taking a step back from the individual projects to see everything that's on your team's plate and deciding what to do with it all. But you need some guiding principles about what work you do need to do.

Those guiding principles—how you define your strategy—start with an actionable mission.

11.1 Define the Business You Are In

Your users—not necessarily your customers—define the business you are in. Your users have problems that your products or systems or deliverables solve for them. You might sell the systems to people who are not your users: think of companies who provide voicemail systems, where the buyers are telephone system administrators but the users are the people who buy telephone system access from the telephone system providers.

---

1. http://www.google.com/corporate/

In order to define your organization's, group's, or team's mission, you have to know what business you're in. The problems your projects solve define the business you are in.

Don't be surprised if the business you are in is *not* the software business. If you provide voicemail systems, you're in the telephony business. If you provide medical records, you're in health care. If you provide embedded systems for process control, you could be in the manufacturing or automobile business, depending on what the embedded systems control.

11.2 What Good Is a Mission, Anyway?

A mission explains what your team, group, or organization does and what work is outside those boundaries. The more tactical (actionable) your mission is, the more the mission helps you draw the boundaries of work that belongs in your group and work that doesn't belong. You know what to do with work that doesn't belong—you put it on the unstaffed work list and work with your manager or your peers to get it off your plate. The more strategic your mission is, the more inspiring it might be, but people might not know how to use the mission to guide their day-to-day work.

Consider these other larger missions. As of September 16, 2008, the Walt Disney Company's mission is to "produce unparalleled entertainment experiences based on the rich legacy of quality creative content and exceptional storytelling."[2]

The bigger the group or organization, the less specific the corporate mission is. I found this statement in JetBlue's customer bill of rights: "Above all else, JetBlue Airways is dedicated to bringing humanity back to air travel."[3] Tesco, a large supermarket chain based in the United Kingdom, says this: "Our core purpose is to create value for customers to earn their lifetime loyalty."[4] ExxonMobil says, "ExxonMobil's primary role—and most important benefit to society—is to safely provide reliable and affordable supplies of energy to people around the world."[5]

---

2. http://corporate.disney.go.com/corporate/overview.html
3. http://www.jetblue.com/about/ourcompany/promise/index.html
4. http://www.tescoplc.com/plc/about_us/values/
5. http://www.exxonmobil.com/Corporate/community_ccr_overview.aspx

> ### Separate Your Personal Mission from the Business
>
> Each of us chose our work for a particular reason—our personal mission. Don't confuse your personal mission with the mission of your team, group, or organization.
>
> Yes, your personal mission must be congruent with the business' mission. I was once called an SQA director, but my management wanted no metrics and no process. I insisted we call the group the Test group and me the Test Director, because we did not do software quality assurance; we did testing. I wasn't happy with that mission, but that's what the company paid me to do.
>
> Your personal mission is what drives *you* to do great work. You need it. Just make sure you keep your personal mission, um, personal. Don't impose your mission on your group. Make sure you're doing what your organization requires.

Regardless of what you think about these organizations, their value statements or missions set some boundaries and guidance for their staff. Given those guiding values, the technical staff on a project or managers responsible for several groups can use those values to guide their work and define their missions.

11.3 Define an Actionable Mission for the Organization

A good mission is actionable: it provides guidance and boundaries for people to use as they work and as they select which work to do.

Your group's mission might be something like "Develop and create high-performance computing systems." But, if you have a sales department out of control, your development manager's mission might be "Be the conscience of the sales department." That manager explained, "We have to do enough prework to know whether we can deliver, in a reasonable amount of time, what sales wants to promise. We want to make it easy for them, so we work in short iterations and predict velocity from what we know."

A test manager told me her group's mission was "Assess the state of the software at any time and report on it." As she said, "That mission gave me ammunition to determine which areas we needed for test automation and the machines we needed."

A program manager with several Scrum teams all working to create a product said his mission was "Ship this product before our competitor ships theirs." Using Scrum, along with many of the XP practices, allowed him to know that the product was always in a done state, so he could keep interrogating the marketing folks about product intelligence to know when they had to ship.

A CIO for a health-care organization said his group's mission was "Create an environment in which people can deliver state-of-the-art health-care solutions." I asked him what "state-of-the-art" meant to him. "Docs get computers that freaking work. The medical records are updated in real time. The people who call in for referrals get them. Same day. None of this "We can't do that referral today" or "We can't renew a prescription until tomorrow. *Today* is what we need." After working with him and his staff, they changed their mission to this: "Deliver working products to medical office staff so they can deliver health care *today*, not tomorrow."

Another test manager told me her mission was "Find the Big Bad Bugs before the customers do." That allowed her group to focus on the risky areas of the products the developers were creating.

A customer service manager told me his mission was "Insulate the CEO from random customer input." His mission allowed him to create a respected group of support staff in an organization known for its developers, not its support staff.

Several development managers have told me their missions are "Provide for the care and feeding of the developers." One development manager said something a little different: "Create an environment in which developers can do good work and grow." For these development managers, it wasn't enough to complete a product; they integrated career development into their missions.

No matter where you are in the organization, make sure your mission is clear, is actionable, and expresses a benefit to someone. If you follow your mission, you will benefit the organization.

> ### Managers: Do Management Work
>
> If you're a senior manager and your mission is to create oppor-
> tunities, does that mean you start projects to create opportu-
> nities? Sure. Does it mean you manage those projects? Almost
> never.
>
> If you're a senior manager, your job is to create a whole-
> organization environment in which people can work well. You
> can't do that if you're trying to manage a project—any project.
> Even if you think it's just a one-person project to investigate
> some possibilities, assign someone from your group to do that
> work and report to you.
>
> If you're a mid-level manager, your job is to create that envi-
> ronment (of enabling great work) for your groups or teams and
> to see other projects or work to build on the higher strategy. If
> you're a first-level manager, your job is to create an environ-
> ment in which your group or team can work, to remove obsta-
> cles, and to consider strategic work that might make your tac-
> tics easier to manage.
>
> As a manager, your most important job is to talk to the con-
> sumers of your projects and see where they are headed. If you
> keep a narrow view of your business, eventually your business
> will go under.
>
> As for nitty-gritty work, you will have plenty to do if you keep up
> with incremental funding, evaluating the portfolio, hiring peo-
> ple, and mentoring and coaching your managers. But it's all
> management work. It's not technical contributor work.

11.4 Draft a Mission from Scratch

An actionable mission contains a verb related to the results of the organization. If you're an airline, a mission might be "Fly people and their
luggage together." If you look back at the missions in Section 11.3,
Define an Actionable Mission for the Organization, on page 149, you can
see that each mission grabs the reader with a strong verb.

To draft a mission with your group without looking at your current
work, try these steps:

1. Brainstorm the mission pieces. Define what you do for whom and
   the value people received from that work.

2. Specify strong verbs.

3. Eliminate adverbs.

4. Iterate until you feel comfortable with the mission.

Don't worry if you can't define your mission in a quick thirty-minute meeting. A team of individual contributors focused on the same goal might be able to define their mission in an hour or two. Once you have several teams, especially if they have varying goals, the mission will be harder to define. The more managers, the harder the mission will be, because they all need to have a mission that supports their work but is greater than any one of them. If you have more than one group, work bottom-up if you have no overall mission. That is, make sure each group develops their mission first and then works to create the greater mission that supports everyone.

11.5 Brainstorm the Essentials of a Mission

If you've never written a mission statement before, try brainstorming the elements of your mission:

1. Invite the members of your group to participate.

2. Give everyone thick markers, blank paper, and plenty of sticky notes.

3. Divide people into smaller working teams of two to three people.

4. Ask people to think about the work they do and then to think of what drives their work. The driver might be the verb.

5. Ask people to think about the boundaries of their work—what's in and what's out.

6. Ask everyone write down these words: the driver, the boundaries. One word to a sticky.

7. Post the stickies on a well so everyone can see all the stickies.

8. Now, ask people to work together in small groups to draft a mission statement.

Once the mission statements are written on stickies, post the statements on the wall, making sure to keep one statement on a line. If you're curious, the picture of "My Mission" on the next page is how I started to write my mission.

Now everyone can review every other group's statements. Encourage the group discussion as people review the stickies. Once people have discussed enough, somewhere between five minutes for teams who really know what they're doing to twenty-five minutes for teams who can't agree, you have a decision. If people really can't agree on the work they need to do, adjourn the meeting for now, and agree to meet in a few days or a week to see whether you can decide then. Between now and then, make sure you aren't asking people who perform different work to try to agree on a mission.

Four Groups, One Manager, Four Group Missions, One Department Mission
by Cheryl, Group Manager

I had a group called Development Services. That meant I had all the testers, writers, release engineers, and continuing engineering as part of one group. I had leads for each of the groups and thought I could write a mission with all of them together for our group. Wrong-o! You never saw such fighting about what we did and didn't do.

First, I had to work with each group to write their mission with them. Once each group had a clear mission (which took just one one-hour meeting), I gathered the leads again and asked that now that they each knew what their mission was, could we work on the department's mission? Piece of cake. But we had to separate the group missions from the department's mission.

This would have been easier if we'd had real managers instead of leads—that would have triggered us all to think a little differently. But we didn't. We finally figured it out.

As people agree on the pieces of the mission, order the stickies so you create a mission statement from the stickies.

11.6 Refine the Mission

Once you have the elements of your mission from the brainstorming, make sure you have strong verbs and have eliminated adverbs and jargon.

11.6.1 Strengthen Your Verbs

Action verbs need to be more than "do." Yes, it is a verb. But it doesn't give you or your group guidance about *what* to do. "Do" is a weak verb. Instead, think about what "do" means. Does it mean "perform" or "obtain" or "create"? It might mean something different, so specify what it means.

Sometimes people use adverbs for emphasis, such as "Really provide real-time answers." Adverbs weaken writing. If you used adverbs to strengthen your sentence or for emphasis, eliminate the adverbs and strengthen the verbs. To see other ways to strengthen your writing, read *On Writing* [Kin00] and *Weinberg on Writing* [Wei05].

For example, if you wrote "Really help," you might mean assist, guide, or facilitate.

11.6.2 Avoid Jargon

Too many missions have words such as "empower" or "make a difference" or "provide superior" products or services. Eliminate those jargon words. If you have a word you can generate through buzzword bingo or from any of the online mission statement generators, return to your brainstorming and define what you mean. Jargon allows you to take shortcuts with your ideas and reduce specificity. But your shortcuts won't help you decide which projects to commit to. Be specific.

11.7 Derive Your Mission from Your Work

You may find brainstorming difficult. In that case, try using your work to help you define your mission.

Ideally, your organization would have an actionable mission that you could use to help define your project's or group's or team's mission. But even if the organization has a great mission, the levels of managers between you and the top may not have created actionable missions for themselves and their groups. In that case, you'll have to derive your mission from your work.

Sometimes, you need to use your work to define your mission, as in "Make Your Mission Possible" [Rot08a]. A colleague explained how he and his group decided their mission when he was tired of his senior management's apparent lack of direction.

My Management Can't Decide What's Important
by Randy, Technical Lead

I was minding my own business, working on a pretty strange problem in the database. My manager, Cindy, walked over and plunked herself down. "Can you add a report to this release? Remember the report we postponed from this release?" I nodded. "It's back in again."

"Look, we took that out for a damn good reason. A few good reasons. One, it doesn't belong in this release. Two, it's not where we want this product to go. It's supposed to go into the next product. Three—"

"I know. But my boss rolled over my objections. I really hate coming to you like this."

"Don't then."

Cindy rolled her eyes. "I have an idea. Let's organize our work in a way that makes sense to us, and then maybe I'll have more ammunition."

We bucketed all the work we had to do and organized a project portfolio around the buckets. It has been more than a year, and Cindy's boss has been listening to her objections and making reasonable decisions.

Here's how to define your mission from your work. First, look back at all the work you collected in Section 3.1, *Know What Work to Collect*, on page 21. Now categorize your work into three buckets:

• Work that seems to make sense for our group

• Work that needs to get done, but maybe not by us

• Work that we are doing but we don't understand why

If you're a development manager, developing systems makes sense for your group. Helping sales or service people with installations is work that needs to be done, but maybe not by you. If someone in the development's group has a role answering the phone as a first-line service tech, that's work you're doing but you don't understand why.

As you collect the work that needs to be done but not by you, think of a group inside the organization that should do this work. If that group exists, create a sticky with the name of that group, and organize the work under that group's name. If there is no group that looks like they should do that work, create another sticky with "We don't understand why we're doing this work."

If you define your mission from your work, make sure you check in with your boss and see whether he or she agrees. You might need to modify your mission—and the work—in order to come to agreement with your boss.

11.8 How to Define a Mission When No One Else Will

I've worked with senior managers and technical leads who worked in organizations that did not have a mission or a strategy. Sometimes those organizations grew quickly and had not paid attention to strategic planning. Sometimes, they suffered from a leadership vacuum at the top, such as no CEO. In any case, your organization doesn't have a mission. But without a mission, you or your managers can't decide what is most important. To protect your team and accomplish anything, you will need to decide. You can use the portfolio and generate a mission based on the work you think is most valuable to the organization.

Make sure you bucket the information as in Section 11.7, *Derive Your Mission from Your Work*, on the previous page. Now, look at the team you have. Look at the work. Use the work you can accomplish to drive your mission building. Is this perfect? Not by a long shot. On the other hand, if you say, "Here is the work we are doing to move the organization forward. If you don't like this, let's change our mission and then reevaluate and rerank the portfolio," then you can at least get some work done that makes sense to your staff and to the rest of the organization.

11.9 Beware of the Mission Statement Traps

As I've worked with managers, I've noticed a number of mission statement traps. The most common is the service-level agreement trap.

11.9.1 The Service-Level Agreement Trap

If you have a lot of emergency projects and you're now trying to manage the portfolio by defining your mission, you're going to start saying no to some work. When you say no, some people are going to tell you that you need to respond more quickly than you are. Or, maybe you feel badly about saying no to some people in the organization. You might even be tempted to set a response time: "We'll finish that in the next twenty-four to forty-eight hours."

Promising a service level for a product development group (development, testing, business analysis, documentation, whatever) is nuts. It guarantees technical debt unless you really can interrupt what you are doing, finish that work, and then restart what you were doing. Your chances of success are minimal.

On the other hand, if you are a group that does some sort of support work (support operations, tier-three customer support), you may want to have some sort of service level for *that* work. Service levels for projects make no sense.

The problem is you are working on projects. Service-level response times interfere with project work and cause multitasking. Maybe someone has to do that work, but maybe not you. Or, if you do have to do it, someone else can rank order the work, and you can work in short timeboxes so you have a chance of completing the necessary-to-the-organization work without multitasking.

It does make sense to provide a date in some relatively short period of time. But remember, software product development is not a service. It is product development (or system development, if you prefer). Support work is problem solving or checklist work. The risk in support work is in the time required to solve the problem. For product development, the risk is in whether you can solve the problem at all, not just in a short time frame.

When leads or managers promise short turnarounds—or as one test manager said, "Test all products as they evolve, 24/7/365"—they create an environment where the people can't succeed. The testers can't learn enough details about the product to be effective, and if there's only eight people "supporting" a technical staff of a few hundred developers, then they are understaffed for all the work.

11.9.2 Some Group Owns Total Responsible for Quality

After the service-level agreement trap, a common trap for software organizations is that one group is "responsible" for quality. That group is usually the testers. They have a mission like this one: "Ensure we release high-quality products."

Testers, no matter what you call them, cannot ensure quality. Testers report on the quality, among other things, of the product. Developers might be able to "ensure quality," if senior managers don't hamstring them. But the real people who ensure quality in an organization are the managers. Those people create an environment in which quality can flourish—or not.

11.9.3 The Mission Statement Is Too Loooong

If you try to be all things to all people—and be tactical when you need to be strategic—your mission statement is too long. Here's a test to know whether your statement is too long. After you develop the mission, ask someone to face away from the stickies or the paper on the wall, and ask that person to tell you the mission statement. This is impossible if you have jargon and adverbs in your mission statement. Iterate and refine the mission.

11.9.4 Mission Statement Has Stretch Goals

Yes, you want to make your mission statement inspiring. But a mission statement is not a place for stretch goals. Make the mission statement believable and achievable. Otherwise, how will you select projects that meet the mission?

One development IT manager had the mission "To be the best in software development" when everyone in the group had just two years or fewer in development. The developers knew they were not the best. And, they knew that the projects they needed to complete were not going to make them be the best in development. That mission was not inspiring for the people to continue to work there. Instead, over the course of a couple of years, each person left to pursue that "best" for himself or herself.

Make the mission statement interesting (inspiring if you can), to the point, and congruent with the organization.

11.10 Test Your Mission

When you've written your mission, test it. Or, if you prefer a test-driven approach, use these questions to drive your mission development:

- Is this mission something the people in this group can do?

- Is this mission something the people in this group have the interest, capabilities, and talent to do?

- Does this mission create opportunities for the group and the organization as a whole?

- Is this mission unique, or does it describe some unique value?

- Is it clear what is inside the scope of this mission, and what is outside the scope?

- Does the mission drive action?

Make sure your mission has an action verb. Make sure it draws boundaries around the work so you can see what work you should be doing and see the work you should not be doing.

If you've worked on the mission alone, make sure you check with the team to test it. You can't know whether you have it all right until you test the mission. Review your mission for traps, and eliminate them.

11.11 Make the Mission Real for Everyone

Middle managers define a more tactical mission based on the organization's mission, especially if your senior management has not defined an actionable mission. You'll need to define a mission with tactical parts. That way, the first-level managers can use your mission to refine theirs.

Inspiring and Tactical Missions Are Tough to Write
by Johanna, SQA and Second-Line Support Manager

I was trying to run two independent groups. To the SQA group that was a test group, I provided all the process work. In addition, I was managing a second-line support group, which took the problems the regular support group couldn't handle. I had two independent groups, not one team. I managed those groups not because it made sense to put them together but because they weren't development. I wanted to describe these two groups in some way that made sense to everyone in the groups as well as the rest of the organization.

I started with each separate team and worked with them to define their missions. The test group used "Assess the state of the product at any time and report on that state." The second-line support group developed this mission: "Become the go-to experts in several areas of the system and respond to problems within four working days."

On the face of it, there's no commonality between the two groups. But both groups provided valuable in-depth expertise for much of the system. In four half-hour chunks over four weeks, we developed a mission for the my group as a whole: "Provide system-level expertise to the development groups."

It was worth taking the time. Our mission was inspiring enough for my two teams and helped explain a little about what we did. It was tactical enough and helped us determine when work was outside of our scope.

If you're in middle management, resist the temptation to use jargon or buzzwords. Take the time to write a real mission for your group, whether they are a variety of teams as mine were or whether they have more commonality.

11.12 Now Try This

- Look at your mission now, whether you are a technical lead, a manager, a middle manager, or a senior manager. Is it actionable? Does it say what's in your purview and what's not?

- If you have a mission at your level, make a date with your peers and develop your joint mission so you know how to work across a department or a whole organization.

- Test your mission to make sure you haven't fallen into any traps.

Chapter 12

Start Somewhere ... But Start

As I was writing this book, one of my reviewers asked, "Can people really do this? What if their senior management has no clue? What if their middle management has no clue?"

Yes. You can do this. You can do this if your senior management has no strategic plan and doesn't know about project portfolio management. You can do this even if your middle management has no clue. Look at what you are able to manage, and use the portfolio to provide direction to your team, finish projects, increase your capacity, and provide better answers to your managers.

You can manage the project portfolio at your level of influence. You can work in timeboxes, finishing complete chunks of work. Or, you can limit the work in progress so you can complete chunks of work. You can decide what to do now, what to do later, and what to put off so you effectively never do it. You can work with your peers and make these decisions so that you as a team can complete projects and release them.

Managing the entire project portfolio is easy when senior management has a strategic plan and manages to that plan. It's not too difficult, if the middle managers understand how to think strategically and tactically even if your senior management isn't so good at strategic planning.

Managing the project portfolio is difficult if you're the only one doing it, no matter what level you are. If you're a first-line manager or a technical lead, you may feel as if you're pushing a boulder uphill.

Remember, you can change yourself. You can change your reactions to the work around you. You can offer an alternative to your colleagues and managers. You can't change anyone else.

As long as you finish work in chunks so other people can see it and use it, you will be successful.

Start with your work, and then work with others. This requires courage, but if you've made it this far, you have plenty.

Chapter 13

Glossary

Agile An iterative and incremental way of working that provides valuable working product at regular intervals. A key aspect of agile, as opposed to an iterative/incremental life cycle, is the expectation that the project team will inspect and adapt as it proceeds in order to improve. For more information, see the Agile Manifesto (http://www.agilemanifesto.org).

Big Visible Chart A chart to keep progress visible. A way to display important information. It does not have to be formal; it has to be easy to see.

Burndown chart A chart that tracks how much work remains on your project and whether you'll hit your deadline.

Burnup chart A chart that tracks how much work remains on your project, how much total work there is on your project, and whether you'll hit your deadline.

Cumulative flow A measure of the work in progress over time compared to total scope.

Incremental life cycle A life cycle where the project team develops features, feature chunks, or MMFs as they choose. That development does not have to be completed in a timebox.

Iteration A time period in which people produce completed work. In agile life cycles, the iteration is a fixed duration, a timebox.

Iterative life cycle A life cycle in which the project team completes pieces of functionality. Some iterative life cycles use timeboxes;

others do not. The idea is that the project team plans to go back and complete the functionality later.

Kanban Literally a visual card. Used in software development as a way to represent a unit of work.

Lean A philosophy of working that shortens the time between the customer request and the delivery of that feature by eliminating sources of waste.

Minimum marketable feature (MMF) Smallest piece of functionality that has value to the customer

Pants on Fire schedule game A schedule game where management cannot decide which project is most important and changes its mind frequently.

Product backlog A list of things that need to be completed for the product.

Project A unique undertaking that involves risk and single deadline.

Project dashboard A form of Big Visible Chart that shows project status.

Project portfolio A ranked list of which projects have which priority for how long.

Program A collection of projects that when released all together deliver significant value.

Road map A list, often by quarter, of which features the organization desires in a product.

ROI Return on investment. If you measure the amount of money obtained from this product divided by the amount of money invested in the development of it, you get ROI.

Running, tested features Features that have passed their acceptance tests.

Queue A sequence of waiting tasks.

Queue length The number of items in the kanban queue.

Serial life cycle A life cycle where the project team first obtains all the requirements and then performs analysis, then design, then code, then integration, and then test.

Split Focus schedule game The schedule game where a person is supposed to multitask.

Sunk cost The money already invested in the project or product.

Timebox A fixed duration of time in which a team commits to completing some work.

User story A form of stating requirements. A user story could be of the form "A <user> can complete some task." Or it could be "As a <user>, I want <to do some task> for <some benefit>."

Velocity A chart that shows how quickly the team is completing features.

Bibliography

[All02]   David Allen. *Getting Things Done: The Art of Stress-Free Pro-ductivity*. Penguin, New York, 2002.

[Bec00]   Kent Beck. *Extreme Programming Explained: Embrace Change*. Addison-Wesley, Reading, MA, 2000.

[Bro95]   Frederick P. Brooks, Jr. *The Mythical Man Month: Essays on Software Engineering*. Addison-Wesley, Reading, MA, anniversary edition, 1995.

[Coh06]   Mike Cohn. *Agile Estimating and Planning*. Prentice Hall, Englewood Cliffs, NJ, 2006.

[DCH03]   Mark Denne and Jane Cleland-Huang. *Software by Numbers: Low-Risk, High-Return Development*. Prentice Hall, Englewood Cliffs, NJ, 2003.

[DeM01]   Tom DeMarco. *Slack: Getting Past Burnout, Busywork, and the Myth of Total Efficiency*. Broadway Books, New York, 2001.

[DL99]   Tom Demarco and Timothy Lister. *Peopleware: Productive Projects and Teams*. Dorset House, New York, second edition, 1999.

[Dru64]   Peter Drucker. *Managing for Results*. Pan Books, London, 1964.

[FBB⁺99]   Martin Fowler, Kent Beck, John Brant, William Opdyke, and Don Roberts. *Refactoring: Improving the Design of Existing Code*. Addison Wesley Longman, Reading, MA, 1999.

[FUP91]   Roger Fisher, William Ury, and Bruce Patton. *Getting to Yes*. Penguin Books, New York, second edition, 1991.

[Gol04]   Eliyahu Goldratt. *The Goal*. North River Press, Great Bar-
             rington, MA, third edition, 2004.

[Hig99]   James A. Highsmith III. *Adaptive Software Development:
             A Collaborative Approach to Managing Complex Systems*.
             Dorset House, New York, 1999.

[JAH02]   Ron Jeffries, Ann Anderson, and Chet Hendrickson.
             Extreme Programming Installed. Addison-Wesley, Reading,
             MA, 2002.

[Ker04]   Joshua Kerievsky. *Refactoring To Patterns*. Addison-Wesley,
             Reading, MA, 2004.

[Kin00]   Stephen King. *On Writing*. Scribner, New York, 2000.

[KLT$^+$96] Sam Kaner, Lenny Lind, Catherine Toldi, Sarah Fisk, and
             Duane Berger. *The Facilitator's Guide to Participatory
             Decision-Making*. New Society Publishers, Gabriola Island,
             BC, 1996.

[KS99]   Jon R. Katzenbach and Douglas K. Smith. *The Wisdom of
             Team: Creating the High-Performance Organization*. Harper-
             Collins Publishers, New York, 1999.

[Lik04]   Jeffrey Liker. *The Toyota Way*. McGraw Hill, New York,
             2004.

[McC96]   Steve McConnell. *Rapid Development: Taming Wild Software
             Schedules*. Microsoft Press, Redmond, WA, 1996.

[Moo91]   Geoffrey A. Moore. *Crossing the Chasm*. Harper Business,
             New York, 1991.

[Ohn88]   Taiichi Ohno. *Toyota Production System: Beyond Large Scale
             Production*. Productivity Press, New York, 1988.

[RD05]   Johanna Rothman and Esther Derby. *Behind Closed Doors:
             Secrets of Great Management*. The Pragmatic Programmers,
             LLC, Raleigh, NC, and Dallas, TX, 2005.

[Rot99]   Johanna Rothman. How to use inch-pebbles when you
             think you can't. *American Programmer*, 12(5):24–29, 1999.
             http://www.jrothman.com/Papers/Howinch-pebbles.html.

[Rot04a]   Johanna Rothman. *Hiring the Best Knowledge Workers,
             Techies, and Nerds: The Secrets and Science of Hiring Tech-
             nical People*. Dorset House, New York, 2004.

[Rot04b]   Johanna Rothman.   Multiprojecting: The illusion of progress.   *stickyminds.com*, 2004.   http://www.stickyminds.com/s.asp?F=S7198_COL_2.

[Rot07]   Johanna Rothman. *Manage It!: Your Guide to Modern Pragmatic Project Management*. The Pragmatic Programmers, LLC, Raleigh, NC, and Dallas, TX, 2007.

[Rot08a]   Johanna Rothman. Make your mission possible. *Better Software*, pages 20–21, March 2008.

[Rot08b]   Johanna Rothman. What lifecycle? selecting the right model for your project. *Cutter IT Journal*, pages 22–27, May 2008.

[Saw07]   Keith Sawyer. *Group Genius: The Creative Power of Collaboration*. Basic Books, Philadelphia, PA, 2007.

[Sch04]   Ken Schwaber.   *Agile Project Management with Scrum*. Microsoft Press, Redmond, WA, 2004.

[SF01]   Robert C. Solomon and Fernando Flores. *Building Trust in Business, Politics, Relationships, and Life*. Oxford University Press, New York, 2001.

[SH06]   Venkat Subramaniam and Andy Hunt. *Practices of an Agile Developer: Working in the Real World*. The Pragmatic Programmers, LLC, Raleigh, NC, and Dallas, TX, 2006.

[SR98]   Preston G. Smith and Donald G. Reinertson.   *Developing Products in Half the Time: New Rules, New Tools*. John Wiley & Sons, New York, second edition, 1998.

[Sta00]   R. Brian Stanfield, ed. *The Art of Focused Conversation, 100 Ways to access Group Wisdom in the Workplace*. New Society Publishers, Gabriola Island, BC, 2000.

[Sur05]   James Surowiecki. *The Wisdom of Crowds*. Anchor, New York, 2005.

[Toc05]   Steve Tockey. *Return on Software: Maximizing the Return on Your Software Investment*. Addison-Wesley, Reading, MA, 2005.

[War07]   Allen C. Ward. *Lean Product and Process Development*. The Lean Enterprise Institute, Inc., Cambridge, MA, 2007.

[Wei92]   Gerald M. Weinberg. *Quality Software Management: Volume 1, Systems Thinking*. Dorset House, New York, 1992.

[Wei94]   Gerald M. Weinberg. *Quality Software Management, Volume 3: Congruent Action*. Dorset House, New York, 1994.

[Wei98]   Gerald M. Weinberg. *Psychology of Computer Programming: Silver Anniversary Edition*. Dorset House, New York, 1998.

[Wei05]   Gerald M. Weinberg. *Weinberg On Writing: The Fieldstone Method*. Dorset House, New York, 2005.

[WJ77]   Bruce W.Tuckman and Mary Ann C. Jensen. Stages of small group development revisited. *Group and Organizational Studies*, 2:419–427, 1977.

[WJ96]   James P. Womack and Daniel T. Jones. *Lean Thinking*. Simon and Schuster, New York, 1996.

Index

The Pragmatic Bookshelf

Available in paperback and DRM-free PDF, our titles are here to help you stay on top of your game. The following are in print as of July 2009; be sure to check our website at pragprog.com for newer titles.

Title	Year	ISBN	Pages
Advanced Rails Recipes: 84 New Ways to Build Stunning Rails Apps	2008	9780978739225	464
Agile Retrospectives: Making Good Teams Great	2006	9780977616640	200
Agile Web Development with Rails, Third Edition	2009	9781934356166	784
Augmented Reality: A Practical Guide	2008	9781934356036	328
Behind Closed Doors: Secrets of Great Management	2005	9780976694021	192
Best of Ruby Quiz	2006	9780976694076	304
Core Animation for Mac OS X and the iPhone: Creating Compelling Dynamic User Interfaces	2008	9781934356104	200
Data Crunching: Solve Everyday Problems using Java, Python, and More	2005	9780974514079	208
Deploying Rails Applications: A Step-by-Step Guide	2008	9780978739201	280
Design Accessible Web Sites: 36 Keys to Creating Content for All Audiences and Platforms	2007	9781934356029	336
Desktop GIS: Mapping the Planet with Open Source Tools	2008	9781934356067	368
Developing Facebook Platform Applications with Rails	2008	9781934356128	200
Enterprise Integration with Ruby	2006	9780976694069	360
Enterprise Recipes with Ruby and Rails	2008	9781934356234	416
Everyday Scripting with Ruby: for Teams, Testers, and You	2007	9780977616619	320
FXRuby: Create Lean and Mean GUIs with Ruby	2008	9781934356074	240
From Java To Ruby: Things Every Manager Should Know	2006	9780976694090	160
GIS for Web Developers: Adding Where to Your Web Applications	2007	9780974514093	275
Google Maps API, V2: Adding Where to Your Applications	2006	PDF-Only	83
Groovy Recipes: Greasing the Wheels of Java	2008	9780978739294	264
Hello, Android: Introducing Google's Mobile Development Platform	2008	9781934356173	200
Interface Oriented Design	2006	9780976694052	240
Land the Tech Job You Love	2009	9781934356265	280
Learn to Program, 2nd Edition	2009	9781934356364	230

Continued on next page

Title	Year	ISBN	Pages
Manage It! Your Guide to Modern Pragmatic Project Management	2007	9780978739249	360
Mastering Dojo: JavaScript and Ajax Tools for Great Web Experiences	2008	9781934356111	568
Modular Java: Creating Flexible Applications with OSGi and Spring	2009	9781934356401	260
No Fluff Just Stuff 2006 Anthology	2006	9780977616664	240
No Fluff Just Stuff 2007 Anthology	2007	9780978739287	320
Practical Programming: An Introduction to Computer Science Using Python	2009	9781934356272	350
Practices of an Agile Developer	2006	9780974514086	208
Pragmatic Project Automation: How to Build, Deploy, and Monitor Java Applications	2004	9780974514031	176
Pragmatic Thinking and Learning: Refactor Your Wetware	2008	9781934356050	288
Pragmatic Unit Testing in C# with NUnit	2007	9780977616671	176
Pragmatic Unit Testing in Java with JUnit	2003	9780974514017	160
Pragmatic Version Control Using Git	2008	9781934356159	200
Pragmatic Version Control using CVS	2003	9780974514000	176
Pragmatic Version Control using Subversion	2006	9780977616657	248
Programming Clojure	2009	9781934356333	304
Programming Erlang: Software for a Concurrent World	2007	9781934356005	536
Programming Groovy: Dynamic Productivity for the Java Developer	2008	9781934356098	320
Programming Ruby: The Pragmatic Programmers' Guide, Second Edition	2004	9780974514055	864
Programming Ruby 1.9: The Pragmatic Programmers' Guide	2009	9781934356081	960
Programming Scala: Tackle Multi-Core Complexity on the Java Virtual Machine	2009	9781934356319	250
Prototype and script.aculo.us: You Never Knew JavaScript Could Do This!	2007	9781934356012	448
Rails Recipes	2006	9780977616602	350
Rails for .NET Developers	2008	9781934356203	300
Rails for Java Developers	2007	9780977616695	336
Rails for PHP Developers	2008	9781934356043	432
Rapid GUI Development with QtRuby	2005	PDF-Only	83
Release It! Design and Deploy Production-Ready Software	2007	9780978739218	368
Scripted GUI Testing with Ruby	2008	9781934356180	192
Ship it! A Practical Guide to Successful Software Projects	2005	9780974514048	224

Continued on next page

Title	Year	ISBN	Pages
Stripes ...and Java Web Development Is Fun Again	2008	9781934356210	375
TextMate: Power Editing for the Mac	2007	9780978739232	208
The Definitive ANTLR Reference: Building Domain-Specific Languages	2007	9780978739256	384
The Passionate Programmer: Creating a Remarkable Career in Software Development	2009	9781934356340	200
ThoughtWorks Anthology	2008	9781934356142	240
Ubuntu Kung Fu: Tips, Tricks, Hints, and Hacks	2008	9781934356227	400

Also by Johanna Rothman

Manage It!

Manage It! is an award-winning, risk-based guide to making good decisions about how to plan and guide your projects. Author Johanna Rothman shows you how to beg, borrow, and steal from the best methodologies to fit your particular project. You'll find what works best for *you*.

• Learn all about different project lifecycles • See how to organize a project • Compare sample project dashboards • See how to staff a project • Know when you're done—and what that means.

Manage It! Your Guide to Modern, Pragmatic Project Management
Johanna Rothman
(360 pages) ISBN: 0-9787392-4-8. $34.95
http://pragprog.com/titles/jrpm

Behind Closed Doors

You can learn to be a better manager—even a great manager—with this guide. You'll find powerful tips covering:

• Delegating effectively • Using feedback and goal-setting • Developing influence • Handling one-on-one meetings • Coaching and mentoring • Deciding what work to do-and what not to do • . . . and more!

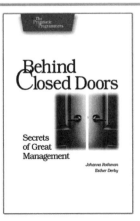

Behind Closed Doors: Secrets of Great Management
Johanna Rothman and Esther Derby
(192 pages) ISBN: 0-9766940-2-6. $24.95
http://pragprog.com/titles/rdbcd

The Pragmatic Bookshelf

The Pragmatic Bookshelf features books written by developers for developers. The titles continue the well-known Pragmatic Programmer style and continue to garner awards and rave reviews. As development gets more and more difficult, the Pragmatic Programmers will be there with more titles and products to help you stay on top of your game.

Visit Us Online

Manage Your Project Portfolio
http://pragprog.com/titles/jrport
Source code from this book, errata, and other resources. Come give us feedback, too!

Register for Updates
http://pragprog.com/updates
Be notified when updates and new books become available.

Join the Community
http://pragprog.com/community
Read our weblogs, join our online discussions, participate in our mailing list, interact with our wiki, and benefit from the experience of other Pragmatic Programmers.

New and Noteworthy
http://pragprog.com/news
Check out the latest pragmatic developments, new titles and other offerings.

Save on the eBook

Save on the eBook versions of this title. Owning the paper version of this book entitles you to purchase the electronic versions at a terrific discount.

PDFs are great for carrying around on your laptop—they are hyperlinked, have color, and are fully searchable. Most titles are also available for the iPhone and iPod touch, Amazon Kindle, and other popular e-book readers.

Buy now at pragprog.com/coupon.

Contact Us

Online Orders:	www.pragprog.com/catalog
Customer Service:	support@pragprog.com
Non-English Versions:	translations@pragprog.com
Pragmatic Teaching:	academic@pragprog.com
Author Proposals:	proposals@pragprog.com
Contact us:	1-800-699-PROG (+1 919 847 3884)